The Encyclopædia
of Stupidity

*Matthijs van Boxsel has been writing and lecturing on stupidity for years.
He lives in Amsterdam.*

Matthijs van Boxsel

The Encyclopædia
of Stupidity

Translated by Arnold and Erica Pomerans

REAKTION BOOKS

Published by Reaktion Books Ltd
79 Farringdon Road
London EC1M 3JU

www.reaktionbooks.co.uk

This is a revised and enlarged edition of *De Encyclopedie van de Domheid*
Copyright © 1999 Matthijs van Boxsel. Amsterdam, Em. Querido's Uitgeverij B. V.

First published 2003
This paperback edition 2004

Translation by Arnold and Erica Pomerans
Translation copyright © Reaktion Books Ltd 2003

This publication has been made possible with financial support
from the Foundation for the Production and Translation of Dutch Literature.

Printed and bound in Great Britain
by Bookmarque Ltd, Croydon, Surrey

British Library Cataloguing in Publication Data
Boxsel, Matthijs van
   The encyclopaedia of stupidity
   1. Stupidity
   I. Title
   153.9

ISBN 1 86189 231 4

Contents

IV The Ha-Ha

V Simpletons in Hell

VI The Genealogy of Dullards

VII On the Inherent Stupidity of Constitutional Monarchies

VIII   The Darwin Awards

INTRODUCTION

On the title-page, in tall angular letters was written the word: stupidities. His eyes rested at first on this. Then he turned over the pages; more than half the notebook was full. Everything he would have preferred to forget he put down in this book. Date, time and place came first. Then followed the incident that was supposed to illustrate the stupidity of mankind. An apt quotation, a new one for each occasion, formed the conclusion. He never read these collected examples of stupidity; a glance at the title-page sufficed. Later on he thought of publishing them under the title 'Morning Walks of a Sinologist'.

Elias Canetti, *Auto-da-Fé*, trans. C. V. Wedgwood (London, 1946)

The Encyclopædia of Stupidity is an enterprise of delirious proportions that was initiated in 1980. The Dutch edition of the book before you appeared in 1999, and served as a general introduction to the subject in which stupidity was cheerfully dissected with the help of cartoons, fairy-tales, triumphal arches, garden designs, baroque ceilings, the House of Orange, pieces of nonsense and science fiction.

In 2001 a second volume was published in The Netherlands. It was entitled *Morosofie* (Foolosophy) and contained the 100 most absurd theories of twentieth-century Dutch thinkers. (Was Delphi Delft? Did abstract thinking start after the clitoris moved from the inside to the outside? Is stupidity the motor of our civilization? How many sheepdog particles does it take to make a sheepdog? Are atoms space-ships?)

The Topography of Stupidity, in which all the European towns and provinces proverbially renowned for their stupidity are catalogued, will appear in due course. Further volumes in preparation will cover stupidity and commerce, stupidity and sexuality, stupidity and art, as well as a theology of stupidity.

Stupidity manifests itself in each walk of life, in every human being, at all times. As a result, any study of stupidity automatically assumes encyclopaedic dimensions.

The true encyclopædist cuts his objects down to size, smoothes away contradictions and systematizes his topics with an iron fist. His work serves the poor in spirit. *The Encyclopædia of Stupidity*, by contrast, allows ample room for conflicting information and criticism.

On the one hand this encyclopædia encompasses etymological analyses, studies of the phenomenon and the theory of stupidity; on the other, it attempts to develop a method for exposing the stupidity of our thinking. The aim is to forge a one-man theory that, in the best of cases, provides an original line of approach to self-evident phenomena.

The obvious move would have been to make my own entreprise the first entry in *The Encyclopædia of Stupidity*, but in view of the capricious nature of the subject I have found it more helpful to follow the *Encyclopédie pittoresque du calembour, recueillie et mise en désordre* par *Joseph Prudhomme* (Picturesque encyclopædia of puns, collected and disorganized by Joseph Prudhomme).

The essays form variations on a recurring theme. Let us hope that – after perusing the book – the reader will be able to hum the tune by heart.

ONE

THE BLACK FLAG

THE ACADEMY OF STUPIDITY

If you pay attention and understand what is said, you will be
wise and happy. If, on the other hand, you do not, you will
become foolish, unhappy, sullen, and stupid, and you will
fare badly in life. For the explanation is similar to the riddle
that the Sphinx used to pose to men: if someone understood
it he was spared, but if he did not understand, he was
destroyed by the Sphinx. It is just the same in the case of this
explanation. You see, for mankind, Foolishness is the Sphinx.
Foolishness speaks in riddles of these things: of what is good,
what is bad, and what is neither good nor bad in life. Thus,
if anyone does not understand these things he is destroyed by
her, not all at once, as a person devoured by the Sphinx died.
Rather, he is destroyed little by little, throughout his entire
life, just like those who are handed over for retribution. But if
one does understand, Foolishness is in turn destroyed, and he
himself is saved and is blessed and happy in his whole life.
As for you, then, pay attention; do not misunderstand.

Tabula Cebetis (2nd century AD), *The Tabula of Cebes*, trans.
John Fitzgerald and L. Michael White (Chico, CA, 1983)

A treadmill turns on a starless plain. A soap bubble is blown along by
the wind. Frogs croak reverently at a crowned log. The meadow smiles.

Imperturbably, the encyclopædist roams through the ever-startling
landscape of stupidity. His watchful eye is cool and unsentimental.
A mule track leads him past vessels filled with lost reason, along a
ha-ha winding through pastureland, past a door without walls. His
specimen box contains a black tulip, a narcissus and a pimpernel.
Having been pricked by a sea holly, he calls on St Tumbo to staunch

Portrait of Matanasius. From *Chef d'œuvre d'un inconnu* (The Hague, 1714)

the blood. He journeys through remote mountain villages, wanders through backward provinces, and dreams of a fool's paradise.

Then he arrives at the Academy of Stupidity. On its roof flutters a black flag that absorbs all light and reflects nothing. Swathed in a cloud, divine Stupidity reads her own history on the frieze around the dome: grinning men dig pits in order to bury the dug-up soil.

In the gallery of the academy, marble statues stand on pedestals, among them a figure wrapped in a cloak of fish scales, a blindfolded woman with a wheel in her hand who is seated on a slope, and a man with a pig's head.

Above the entrance hangs Stupidity's coat of arms: a shield emblazoned with a pair of bellows and supported by a peacock and an ass. A parrot nests in the crown. Stained glass depicts a sphinx, with below it the question:

Who is clever enough to fathom his own stupidity?

Portrayed on the walls of the entrance hall, an anonymous rabble, pursued by hornets and wasps, rushes after a fluttering ensign. By way of the monumental stairwell, where Prudentia is gazing into a mirror, the inspector of stupidity enters a circular hall. Its enormous vault is supported by mythological fools: several Giants, Cyclops, Epimetheus, King Midas and a man with a pebble in his mouth. An apotheosis of stupidity is painted on the high ceiling in such manner that the roof appears to be crashing down.

On the wall hangs a map of the world, with hundreds of small flags marking such proverbially stupid towns as Gotham, Schilda and Kampen. Next to the Amersfoort erratic boulder lies an Irish mug with its handle on the inside, together with a loose screw.

On a calendar, 1 April and 11 November have been circled, and so have all Wednesdays, the Fornacalia in February, the name day of St Polycarp and that of St Matthijs (or Matthew), the intercalary day on which one is allowed to be delirious. Astrological signs have been scribbled in the margin; anyone born in May or under the sixteenth degree of Leo is destined to be a fool.

The floor is strewn with craniometric instruments, a model of the hollow earth, and maps of Atlantis, Utopia and Lemuria. There are labels everywhere bearing legends, dates or diagrams.

A path guides the visitor past the flora and fauna of stupidity: a goose in a cage, an owl on a branch, a fish in a glass bowl. A bat flies through the room. A headless chicken runs about. The backside of a pig can be seen protruding from under a red curtain embroidered with a crown in gold thread. The pig and other beasts (most of them edible and domesticated) populate the zoological garden of stupidity, a *bestiarium stupidum*. The walk continues past a clump of poppies, some brambles, a maple, a potted geranium and a container with a small almond tree. Along the way, the visitor passes a sofa on which a dumb blonde is ogling a he-man. In the background a small choir is singing *Stupid Cupid*, a cappella. Finally the visitor reaches the library of stupidity. A wooden wigmaker's head serves as a bookend for several standard works on stupidity including:

> *Von der Wollust der Dummheit*
> *The Anatomy of Error*
> *Der Begriff der Dummheit bei Thomas von Aquin und seine*
>   *Spiegelung in Sprache und Kultur*
> *La folie dans la raison pure*
> *Über die Dummheit. Eine Umschau im Gebiete menschlicher*
>   *Unzulänglichkeit. Mit einem Anhange: Die menschliche*
>   *Intelligenz in Vergangenheit und Zukunft*
> *Le leggi fondamentali della stupidità umana*
> *Die Onomasiologie der Dummheit*

A separate bookcase contains *Psittacisme*, a learned tome on the mindless parroting of other peoples' speech. It leans against a series of reference works in which the language of stupidity is recorded – *sottisiers* and *bêtisiers* full of garbled sentences, glib opinions and clichés. The spine of a thick volume reads *Press* and *Broadcasting*. Leafing through it we discover such pronouncements as:

- 'You can't make an omelette without frying eggs'
- 'This is a real feather in the cap of our welfare state'
- 'The prospects sound too rosy to me'
- 'We've only one person to blame and that's each other'
- 'Youth Hit By Train Is Rushed To Two Hospitals'
- 'Foreign investors are descending on Hong Kong like bees on a honey pot, all looking for a piece of the pie'

On towering stacks of filing cabinets lie a Nuremberg funnel, used by teachers to cram information into recalcitrant pupils, a hat made of lead and a small box of children's nail clippings. Tabs impose military order on the rank and file of the boxed index cards. Once something is placed in the archives of stupidity, it is not easy to get it out again . . .

Then there is a collection of gramophone records by such musicians as Lou Reed (*Stupid Man*), Dolly Parton (*Dumb Blonde*), Frank Zappa (*Dumb All Over*), Graham Parker (*The Museum of Stupidity*) and the unforgettable Alvaro Amici with his *Roma, nun fa la stupida stasera*. The morosopher sits at his cembalo and plays Rameau's uncle's *Les niais de Sologne*. A TV set in the middle of the hall provides a view of the world. Canned laughter pours out at full pelt.

THE DISCOVERY

> During his medical examination a conscript picks up all the
> pieces of paper he can find, repeating over and over again,
> 'That's not it. That's not it.' The psychiatrist decides he is
> insane and issues him with an exemption certificate. The
> conscript looks at the certificate and says, 'That's it!'

While in search of a subject on which I could concentrate with all my might, a subject that, moreover, would make the most extreme demands on me, I took cognizance of everything I encountered, like someone who is in love but does not know with whom. I assembled amusing collections of items connected with the quail (*Coturnix dactylisonans*), triumphal arches, and the *Ardalio* (an actor whose sole role was to walk unceasingly up and down the stage). By way of illustration of my vain attempts to bring some order into my life, I even spent many years cataloguing newspaper cuttings that used the red-thread metaphor. A random selection from the thousands of quotations:

> With the cocoa bean as his *red thread*, he is about to write an
> account of the North–South relationship in Ghana.

> Rain goes with Wimbledon like strawberries and cream,
> salmon sandwiches, gin and tonic, ticket touts, grass courts,

and, during the past few decades, bomb threats. Like a *red thread*, bad weather runs through the history of the world's leading tennis tournament.

The production has been put at risk by the ten days we have lost through disputes, something we are now trying to make up for. We always get there in the end, because the *red thread* running through our work is characteristic of all art: just make a start and something is bound to happen. However, we are working up towards a climax, towards a final monumental visual image.

In his mosaic of everyday events, the author has treated last year's most important news like a *red thread*: the fall of the Berlin wall, the Romanian revolution, the release of Nelson Mandela.

Success is the *red thread* running through the entire conference. Success stemming purely from the will to succeed and to gain the 'unqualified support' of the other Taoists in the support group. The secret is to do nothing. 'If you feel like doing something, sit down, take a deep breath, and wait for the urge to pass.'

The history of church fabrics runs like a *red thread* through Christianity.

In the meantime I had discovered the work of the Austrian writer Robert Musil. After reading *The Man Without Qualities*, I threw myself enthusiastically into the rest of his collected writings. In 1980 I read *Über die Dummheit* (On Stupidity), the last text published during his lifetime, a transcript of an address he gave in Vienna in 1937, one year before the Anschluss. The idea that, in addition to wisdom, truth and beauty, stupidity, too, could be a subject of serious study, came to me as a surprise. I was fascinated, the more so as Musil did not define stupidity as a lack of intelligence, but as a lack of feeling. Musil even spoke of intelligent stupidity.

Until then I had dedicated myself obsessively to researching such exalted subjects as melancholy, decadence and the uncanny. Suddenly

I was being confronted with laxity, kitsch and superstition, subjects from which I normally keep aloof. On closer examination, however, they turned out to be the banal flip side of my obsessions. The deadly serious, the high ideal and the hankering after mysteries were suddenly corrected with humour, fallacy and paradox. Stupidity turned up unexpectedly and yet as if to order.

Moreover the subject was suited like no other to relativizing the modish academic preoccupation with differences, boundaries and the Other. With childish delight, I replaced certain words with 'stupidity', whereupon the most boring texts suddenly turned into sources of inspiration. In this way, moreover, the sophistic character of many arguments was made manifest.

Thus my frustrated quest ended in the study of its own failure; in retrospect I came to understand that my mania for collecting, my pedantry and persistent need to be the wittiest of all at any cost, were so many attempts to come to terms with stupidity. The blind rage and paralysing shame I felt at my own stupidity and that of others were revealed as the mainsprings of my existence. It was high time I seized the donkey by the ears.

THE PROFILE OF STUPIDITY

'You're a nobody if you're useless to yourself and to others. Everybody ought to have a function.'
'A function? I've got a function,' replied Jacques.
'Which one?'
'Inspector of human follies, and I don't know anyone who's as busy as I am.'

Eugene Nus, *Nos Bêtises* (1882)

In search of the sources on which Musil drew, I came across a series of serious, often unintentionally comic, studies of stupidity, written by theologians, philosophers, sociologists and physicians. The relevant books quickly grew into a small library. I filed and indexed all definitions of stupidity, and discovered to my surprise that it was generally described not as a failing but as a force.

That view is confirmed by a host of allegories found in medieval and Renaissance prints, in which Stupidity (*Stultitia*) is assigned a special

18

Portrait of Matanasius. From *Chef d'œuvre d'un inconnu* (The Hague, 1714)

place among all the other qualities. Thus we see a woman with bared breasts, a chaplet of narcissi woven in her hair, leaning against a goat that is chewing some sea holly (*eryngo*). The narcissi refer to the Greek word *narkè*, meaning numbness (think of narcosis). According to Pliny, goats refused to be budged after they had chewed eryngo. The bare breasts indicate shamelessness. In this allegory (see my title-page) taken from H. K. Poot's *Het Groot Natuur-en Zedekundigh Werelttoneel* (The Great Natural and Moral World Theatre, 1743), three aspects of stupidity are succinctly addressed: dullness, obstinacy and shamelessness.

A print from Jacob Cats's emblem book *Zinne- en minnebeelden* (Allegories and Depictions of Love) forms a pendant to the above work. We see a woman bearing a book and palm, accompanied by a figure with eagle's wings and an owl's head. Fool's bells dangle from her arms and legs, and she brandishes a 'slapstick', a fool's sceptre with a small bag

Pure and impure birds.
Erhard Schön, woodcut (*c.* 1534)

The screech owl in the day is blind
And so as well is all mankind
Which, blinded to the word of God,
In utter darkness stray and plod.'
Max Geisberg and Walter Leopold
Strauss, *The German Single-Leaf*
Woodcut, 1500–1550 (1975)

of peas used to hit people on the head. In many parts of Western Europe, the owl is a symbol of stupidity, because it is blind and helpless during the day. Think also of the Dutch word *uilskuiken*, meaning owlet as well as numbskull, or the saying 'When the owl sings, the nightingale holds her peace'. In this print, stupidity is not characterized by dullness but by rash behaviour. Wisdom, by contrast, hastens slowly.

In short, stupidity is associated with extremes: she is either too sluggish or too quick. Since the end of the eighteenth century, the emphasis has increasingly been shifted to the kind of stupidity that is associated with mediocrity. The stupid citizen takes front stage not only in engravings but also in literature. One has only to think of Chrysostomus Matanasius, Monsieur Prudhomme, Tribulat Bonhomet, Bouvard, Pécuchet and Batavus Droogstoppel.

Unlike the fools of medieval satire, who exemplified the vices rife around them, the burgher symbolizes the bigoted righteousness of the masses. This philistine sins by not sinning. Compared with his anxiety-ridden opportunism, the deliberate adoption of stupidity assumes an ethical dimension. Normality suddenly looks sick.

It was no accident that in the eighteenth century stupidity was also discovered by phrenologists and craniometrists, who maintained that you could measure intelligence by rule and compass. With paranoid zeal they considered even the most ordinary outward appearance as an expression of a distorted psyche. Their research assumed grotesque forms. Thus they claimed that a fool could be identified even at dusk by his silhouette . . . provided he was bald.

Silhouette of a fool.
From J. C. Lavater,
Over de physiognomie
(Amsterdam, 1784)

'Two more foolish faces whose foreheads bear the signs of natural stupidity, though not to the same extent as the two preceding examples. Both display a degree of obstinacy. The forehead of the first is too high and too narrow; that of the second too thick and too broad. — As to the lower half of the faces, one seems benevolent, the other malevolent. Both may already be identified as fools from the atony of their muscles.'

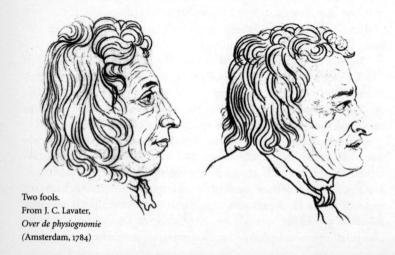

Two fools.
From J. C. Lavater,
Over de physiognomie
(Amsterdam, 1784)

Animal supplement.
From J. C. Lavater,
Over de physiognomie
(Amsterdam, 1784)

1. Noble , proud , courageous , bold.

2. Quite noble , though not of the noblest kind.

3. Porcine , false , ignoble , mulish , sluggish.

4. Of average character , neither sluggish nor submissive — yet neither noble nor great , fiery rather than noble , wild rather than great.

5. Of the same character , but weaker.

6. Treacherous and false.

The profiles sketched by science look suspiciously like the caricatures of satire. One step further is the classification of horses based on outward signs of stupidity and intelligence.

The Encyclopædia of Stupidity begins at the point where the science of stupidity can no longer be distinguished from the stupidity of science.

THE TERRARIUM

Suddenly, the world of stupidity opened up before me, a realm that is very much of this Earth. Its co-ordinates criss-cross those of our daily existence. But in fact it is an independent universe with a flora and fauna of its own, its own language, its own topography and an independent existential principle. I felt like a god surveying his terrarium. If I should so desire, I could engineer a minor Fall of Man.

Still lacking was a logic, an ethic and an aesthetic of stupidity. In the first version of *The Encyclopædia of Stupidity*, a tentative start was made. I refrained from choosing a fixed starting-point, and confined myself instead to partial solutions. 'What drives us on is the secret pleasure every thought provides once it is thought. We order without attaining order.' From the outset I maintained that essays alone can measure up to the unpredictable whims of stupidity. 'Essays justify the subjective choice of a particular approach, and of the often arbitrary arguments needed for venturing into the realm of stupidity, where chance, ambivalence and the principle of insufficient reason reign supreme.'

Interim reports on these researches have been published in three volumes. In 1986 there appeared an *Introduction* as well as a Dutch translation of Musil's *On Stupidity*. In the third volume, published in 1988, an attempt was made to develop a systematic study of stupidity on the basis of Flaubert's letters.

The fourth volume was intended to cover the 'Topography of Stupidity'. It was planned as a simple treatise, in which all the towns in The Netherlands renowned for their stupidity were catalogued, together with the stupidities attributed to them. But then I wondered for the first time rather naïvely why, in fact, these towns were considered to be stupid. I was opening a door that it would have been best to have left shut for the time being. Since the answers I found in the literature did not satisfy me, I searched for a solution of my own, and that kept me busy for ten years. For fear of losing touch with the outside world, I delivered a host of lectures to such aliens as gynaecologists, crisis managers and patent attorneys, and attempted to test the provisional results of my studies. The ultimate aim was a theory into which all the collected definitions of stupidity could be fitted – an original, genuine, would-be philosophy.

The present book is the result of this quest.

THE PREMISE

My starting point is a quip: no man is intelligent enough to grasp his own stupidity. It recalls I Corinthians 3:19: 'For the wisdom of this world is foolishness with God.' Man, by contrast, cannot comprehend the stupidity of his intellect without going mad. According to Erasmus, insight is reserved for those who can step outside themselves, for fools in Christ and ecstatic mystics.

The only fruitful solution is a reversal of perspective: intelligence is nothing but the result of a series of more or less unsuccessful attempts to come to grips with stupidity. And perhaps stupidity is nothing but the externalisation of our abortive attempts to define intelligence . . .

THE DESIGN

The Encyclopædia of Stupidity is not a systematic attempt to present arguments according to a fixed plan. It consists instead of a series of essays, each intended to throw light on the rest. The main premise of the book, that culture is the result of a series of more or less unsuccessful attempts to come to terms with stupidity, continues to crop up in different contexts. The approach is cyclical rather than linear. The essays shed light on the premise from various angles. Because the build-up is not the result of an inevitable development, the argument reaches no conclusion but simply breaks off. In that way, the book illustrates its own argument. *The Encyclopædia of Stupidity* is the product of a series of more or less unsuccessful attempts to understand stupidity. In order to fail as colourfully as possible, the essays are by turn analytical, ironic and aggressive.

To prevent any misunderstanding: unlike the adherents of perspectivism who still believe in an (unattainable) essence, I do not delude myself into thinking that stupidity exists outside the vain efforts to entrap it.

Like every encyclopædia, the present book contains many photographs and other illustrations. In the best case, the argument and the illustrations complement each other to provide a refreshing perspective. The same is true of the accompanying captions. In the belief that all our cultural achievements are successful blunders, I have culled my examples not only from philosophy but also from animated cartoons. The essay is the ideal medium for experimenting with someone else's discoveries. I have not set out to interpret the world; rather have I used the world with its gardens, books, princes and road accidents as an illustration of my approach. The whole of creation is there to prove me right – even if I am wrong.

On the one hand I have drawn inspiration from such standard works as Robert Burton's *The Anatomy of Melancholy*, Baltasar Gracián's *Oráculo Manuel* (The Oracle) and Hans Vaihinger's *Die Philosophie des Als Ob* (The Philosophy of As-If); on the other hand I have benefited from the writings of G. K. Chesterton, J. P Guépin and Slavoj Žižek, to mention a few of the books I have devoured. 'Le lion est fait de mouton digéré' – the lion is made from digested sheep – but who knows whether asses have an equally strong stomach . . .

SHAGREEN

The Encyclopædia of Stupidity is broad enough to make room for all writings on stupidity, including itself. Inspired by Elsevier's *Vogelgids* (Bird Guide) of 1965, which is perversely covered in imitation snake-skin, I have had several copies of the encyclopædia bound in ass's hide, to emphasize the stupidity of the whole project.

THE PEEPSHOW

> For he by Geometrick scale
> Could take the size of Pots of Ale;
> Resolve by Sines and Tangents straight,
> If Bread or Butter wanted weight;
> And wisely tell what hour o' th' day
> The Clock does strike, by Algebra.
>
> Samuel Butler, *Hudibras* (1678)

Research has been done into the effect of side winds on arithmetic sums, into the specific gravity of a kiss, and into the surface of God. There is a statistics of tickling, a *Dialektik des Nichtwissens* (Dialectic of Ignorance) and a study on the influence of fishtails on sea's waves.

Other experts have classified sunsets, developed a mimetic theory based on parrot calls, or attempted to define the orange in terms of vitamins, minerals, fibres, colours and gustatory qualities, volume, girth, and so on.

Why are these studies so fascinating, so absurd and at the same time so heartwarming? Not so much because they are parodies of science, but simply because they are faithful imitations of the folly inherent in all our attempts to come to grips with life. All these amusing treatises hint at the secret enjoyment buried under scientific earnestness, at the childish pleasure of reducing the cosmos to a formula and the world to a peepshow.

Moreover, these monomaniacal studies lend consistency to our life. By concentrating with all our might on a single aspect of existence, however stupid, we can amass the most fantastic store of knowledge and take pleasure in doing so.

The Encyclopædia of Stupidity, too, defends the indefensible but has a more megalomaniac design. There is some danger that my peepshow may assume the dimensions of the world at large.

Should I die before my time, I would like to leave a trunk full of peculiar books, a bizarre collection of pictures and an awe-inspiring quantity of index cards. In one way or another I have always dreamed of finding such a trunk one day.

THE VANISHING HANDKERCHIEF

> I am a member of a magic circle, The Secret Six, which is so
> secret that I don't know the other five.
> Tommy Cooper

During one of his acts, the English conjurer Tommy Cooper would make a blue handkerchief vanish in his left hand, only to make it reappear again from his right jacket pocket. Ignoring professional etiquette, he gave the secret of 'The Vanishing Handkerchief' away to his audiences by repeating the trick in slow motion. Very painstakingly, he would push a blue handkerchief into his left fist, blow on it and perform a bit of hocus-pocus. Meanwhile, an assistant waiting in the wings would walk up, pull the handkerchief out of Cooper's hand, push it into Cooper's right jacket pocket, and disappear again into the wings. After performing a few clumsy dance steps, Cooper would then pull the handkerchief out of his pocket. While the audience applauded, he would say, '*Ttthhhaaannnkkk yyyooouuu.*'

Cooper clearly illustrates the way in which I propose to reveal the hidden role stupidity plays in our world: not by breaking taboos, but by driving home the mystifications involved.

WELL-TRODDEN PATHS

Anyone in search of stupidity must not eschew commonplaces, on the contrary. The point is to present them in a fresh context. We seek adventure along well-trodden paths.

TWO

The Blunderers' Club

THE KNIGHT IN THE BOG

A knight took up arms against Stupidity, a monster no living soul could describe. Only its name and its lair were known. Clad in heavy armour and with sword drawn, the knight waded through the morass. The nearer he came to the haunted place, the deeper his feet sank into the mire. Just before he vanished, the flummoxed knight was embraced by the bog.

THE TOPOLOGY OF STUPIDITY

Stupidity is unfathomable; it can only be defined negatively, by contrast with another quality or as a defect. That does not mean that stupidity does not exist. We see the effects of it every day all around and inside us, but we are always too late to pin it down. Stupidity is a frontier we invariably miss – only in retrospect do we realize that we have crossed it. All we can see is a stultiform void. Meanwhile stupidity itself has never been located. But how can you pinpoint a 'creature' that lacks a place of its own, that is atopic, arcane, absurd?

There is a danger that we create stupidity by defining it, while stupidity lies in the difference. Stupidity is always somewhere else. Once defined and named, it loses its baffling quality. Stupidity recognized is an additional bit of wisdom.

All we can do is to put up road signs pointing to dangerous locations.

ROAD SIGNS

Two roadmen taken on not long ago in the village of Gotham,

renowned for the reputed simplicity of its inhabitants, were given orders to remove all the road signs from a forest that had just been cleared. When the job was done, one of the men wondered how they would ever find their way home. The other told him reassuringly not to worry; after all, they were carrying all the road signs.

THE FATAL COMBINATION

When I speak of stupidity, I am not talking about jesters, or of those who are ill or uneducated human beings. Nor do I have in mind the eccentric who behaves differently from the crowd – quite the contrary. The stupidity that interests me concerns the rule rather than the exception. I am referring to the stupidity characteristic of people in general, a stupidity that is in fact a necessary part of our development.

Stupidity is an aesthetic category; etymologically speaking, the words for stupidity in most languages refer to defects of the senses. The Middle Dutch *domp* or *domb* rubs shoulders with the Middle High German *tump*, *tumb*, *tum*, the Gothic *dumbs*, the Old High German *tump*, the Old Saxon *dumb*, and the High German *dumf*. There is probably a link with the stem of the Dutch *doof* (deaf). The original meaning is 'dumb' (*mutus*), a word we still use as a synonym for 'lacking the faculty of speech' as well as for 'stupid'. Think also of such compounds as shortsighted, thickheaded and dull-witted. Hence the definition of stupidity as a lack of intelligence; a defect of the head was believed to imply a defect in the head. Sensory disorders are thought to influence the perception of reality. Or vice-versa: the external defect is seen as a symptom of an inner weakness.

Etymologies are generally off target. And this etymology, too, leads us down a false trail, for stupidity is no defect. Stupidity is an independent quality with a logic all its own. Those who look for stupidity in the field of the intellect will at best grow a little wiser about the limits of their own intelligence, but learn nothing about the vast land of stupidity on the other side.

Stupidity is not the converse of intelligence; it is the converse of a lack of stupidity, while intelligence is the converse of a lack of intelligence. Particularly fatal is the combination of stupidity and intelligence.

THE PRINCIPLE OF THE WOODCUTTER OUT ON A LIMB

He who thinks great thoughts, errs greatly.

Martin Heidegger

For centuries the world has been full of tales illustrating the problematic relationship between stupidity and intelligence. These so-called epic farces are often attributed to the inhabitants of proverbially stupid places. That is why they are frequently referred to, in accordance with their geographic background, as *Boeotiana* (after Boeotia, a region of ancient Greece renowned for its stupidity), or as Gothamic jests, *Schildbürgerstreiche* (Swabian pranks) or *Kamper uien* (Kampen jokes).

A classic joke concerns a woodcutter out on a limb. He saws off the branch he is sitting on. Intelligence is the art of selection. The man has chosen a sensible task: to separate the branch from the tree. The choice of means, too, is excellent: his saw is sharp. So the job is successfully completed, by the woodcutter breaks his neck. Without intelligence, his stupidity would not have had such a disastrous effect. Fools are dangerous precisely because they are intelligent, because they usually succeed in what they set out to do. And the more intelligent they are, the more catastrophic the consequences of their stupidity.

The fact that stupidity is rarely, if ever, found where we expect it, is demonstrated in a newspaper report published several years ago: a man climbed into a crooked tree to saw off a branch that was smashing his roof tiles. He did not make the classical mistake, but sat close to the trunk. Once free of the heavy branch, however, the tree whipped upwards and the man was catapulted out of it. Once again intelligence proved fatal to a fool.

Stupidity is the talent of acting unwittingly against your own best interests, with death as the ultimate consequence. On the one hand, stupidity poses a threat to our civilization; on the other, stupidity is the mystical foundation of our existence: culture is nothing but the result of a series of more or less unsuccessful attempts to come to terms with our self-destructive folly. Stupidity has forced man to develop his intelligence.

Tragicomically, the woodcutter reveals the stupidity behind all our actions, the most successful included.

THE NOT TERRIBLY GOOD CLUB

In 1976, the Not Terribly Good Club of Great Britain was established in London by Stephen Pile, author of *The Book of Heroic Failures*. The club fell victim to its own success: too many people were keen to join. To be eligible for membership you had to be not terribly good at something. Evenings were held at which people gave demonstrations of their ineptitude. For artists, there was a Salon des Incompétents. On the opening night of Pile's club, a banquet was laid on at a specially chosen second-rate restaurant. When a waitress dropped a bowl of soup by accident, the chairman caught it. Because he averted a disaster, he was expelled from the club on the spot.

So ends the introduction to Stephen Pile's book, but it is here that my own interest begins: preventing a blunder turned out, when seen in the proper light, to have been the greatest blunder of all. For that reason alone, the chairman should have been made honorary life president, dismissed again immediately, then re-appointed, and so on. Imagine that all our blunders were unrecognized successes! And imagine that all our successes were unrecognized blunders!

THE AMSTERDAMMER

> Amsterdam, that grand old town,
> Is built on piles so great
> That should the city tumble down,
> We all would share its fate.

What is an Amsterdammer? An Amsterdammer is anyone who is called an Amsterdammer. The very name breathes life into the Amsterdammer. But that is by no means the whole story. Every Amsterdammer relates to something special that is, by definition, incomprehensible to outsiders. You know it or you don't – it can't be explained. The point is of course that this mysterious core owes its existence to the ignorance of others. But even the Amsterdammer himself hasn't the faintest notion of what it is all about.

Amsterdammership spreads discord among the inhabitants over the question of who is the true Amsterdammer. Hence Amsterdammership keeps Amsterdammers from becoming Amsterdammers.

That is self-destructive stupidity. But at the same time this idiocy is an existential condition, because arguing about his identity defines the true Amsterdammer. Hence there is no point in saying that there are no true Amsterdammers; an Amsterdammer exists exclusively in his failure to behave like one. He only flourishes in the space separating him from himself as an Amsterdammer. An Amsterdammer is a typical Amsterdammer in the surprise, the doubt that spurs him on to act as an Amsterdammer. He is an Amsterdammer in the canals, flags, songs, barrel organs, buildings and other more or less monumental signs of his impotence to come to terms with his Amsterdammership. He is an Amsterdammer in his boasting, in his endless sequence of colourful, but abortive, attempts to prove that he is an Amsterdammer. That is why the greatest Amsterdammers invariably come from outside Amsterdam. The Netherlands is the capital of Amsterdam, and the province of Friesland is a neighbourhood in the suburbs . . .

A born Amsterdammer, by contrast, does not have to prove himself as such; he contributes nothing to the identity of Amsterdam. Strictly speaking, he is redundant – one reason why Amsterdammers migrate en masse to the countryside. There they busy themselves obsessively with the protection of barns, brent geese and greenery, in short with everything that contributes to the cosy rural identity.

EGGSHELLS OF IGNORANCE

In Friesland there is a *stupa*, a temple with a seated bodhisattva, a monk who has attained enlightenment. He is about to enter nirvana. What is stopping him, though? Here we stumble upon the moral para-dox of Mahayana Buddhism. The problem is that the bodhisattva must never enter nirvana unaccompanied, since in doing so he would be vaunting his egoism. Now, if he is an egoist, he cannot be a bodhisattva and hence cannot enter nirvana; if he is a true bodhisattva he cannot enter nirvana because that would be an egoistic act. In short, no one can enter nirvana; ordinary mortals are debarred because they are no bodhisattvas, and bodhisattvas because they are bodhisattvas. (Arthur Danto, *Mysticism and Morality*, New York, 1972)

The bodhisattva's dilemma is like that of the arhat, the sacred hero of Hinayana Buddhism, a branch, which is sometimes condescendingly referred to as the 'Little Vehicle'. An arhat is a monk who has walked the

Eightfold Path and stands on the threshold of absolute peace. With wisdom he has broken the 'eggshells of ignorance' – liberation from all ties to the 'I' and to 'mine' is the prerequisite of salvation. The problem is that his personal search for release from the self is a sign of egoism. And so the arhat himself stands in the way of his own salvation.

Mahayana Buddhism, the so-called Great Vehicle, tries to get over this moral paradox by striving for universal salvation, whence the adjective 'great'. Personal salvation can only be found in the salvation of all. The bodhisattva endeavours to lose himself by transcending all bounds through an infinite extension of the self. No one is saved until everyone is saved. But this search, too, is doomed to come to nothing.

The bodhisattva tries to save mankind, not by performing good deeds, but by setting an example. The statue of the bodhisattva shows us a serene, inward-looking man. The startling difference between his imperturbability and our hectic existence is meant to inspire us to break out of our insane world. Instead, he merely confirms our invincible weakness.

The only thing the bodhisattva can do is to postpone his own salvation until all mankind has attained enlightenment. But by doing that he demonstrates that he himself is an enlightened person. He is a true Buddha in the vain attempt to become a Buddha. He succeeds through failure.

The bodhisattva in the Frisian landscape points by his unruffled presence to our shortcomings and grants us a foretaste of the unimaginable bliss of nirvana. We must see both in the same context. There is no bliss outside the many foolish attempts to reach it.

NO PLEASURE WITHOUT PAIN

> I learned my greatest lessons
> from the distress of others.
> Menander, *Sententiæ*

A man wants to shut a door, walks up to it and shuts it. This is a classic example of a successful, intentional action. Such actions must satisfy three conditions:

There must be the intention to perform the action successfully
The task must be performed successfully
The intention to perform the task successfully is the cause of its
   successful completion.

But consider the following case: a man sets out to shut a door, stumbles, falls against it, and it shuts. The intention is the cause of the
accomplishment of the task; without that intention the man would not
have stumbled, and without stumbling he would have been unsuccessful. But the manner in which he accomplished the task cannot possibly
be called intentional. His success was a stupid accident.

All of us dwell in the confused realm of beneficial blunders, of
actions that succeed because of their failure. We operate in the area that
lies between wise intention and mere fluke. And that lends an unintentionally comic aspect to all our actions. Every action that crosses the
threshold of possibility and is realised in the full sense of that word,
contains at bottom an element of idiocy (Slavoj Žižek, *Le plus sublime
des hystériques*, Paris, 1988).

THE FLUKE

An action that ends, inadvertently and unwittingly, in the desired
result, is called a stroke of luck or a fluke. Morology, the study devoted to the laws of stupidity, draws a distinction between flukes whose
idiotic causes lie beyond the intellect and flukes whose causes lie
within it.

The following is a fluke of the first kind: a man sets out to shoot
another. He misses, but the shot startles a herd of wild boar, which
trample the victim to death. (Donald Davidson, *Essays on Actions and
Events*, Oxford, 1980) Another apt example can be found in the film
A Fish Called Wanda, in which the murderer aims his gun at an old
woman but by accident shoots her little dog, which quite literally breaks
the old woman's heart.

As for a fluke of the second kind: a murderer drives to the home of
his intended victim. In a nervous state, he runs somebody over who
turns out to be his intended victim.

These examples of productive stupidity are not marginal phenomena
but spectacular variants of a form of folly at work in the centre of what

we consider to be our reasonable 'system' of thought. In a blundering way, the stupid mechanics that keeps the world revolving are laid bare.

ADVERSITY AND WISDOM

Quae nocent docent

Adversity makes men wise, as the proverb puts it. This expression, which apparently serves to console losers, in fact reveals the secret logic of our intellect. Wisdom can only be attained through adversity. But of course, this only works at an unconscious level. We must try not to emulate the peasant who banged his head against the wall in an attempt to knock some sense into it. Anyone who deliberately blunders to attain wisdom is a fool. Wisdom can only be gained as the unintended side effect of our actions, as an accidental bit of luck born of a stupid accident.

THE RETROACTIVE EFFECT

Oh Magoo, you've done it again!

We seek wisdom without knowing what it really is. However, our quest for unattainable wisdom leads to the adversity by which we grow wise. Or rather, the wisdom we seek in vain is created only retrospectively by the act of failure itself. That effect accordingly produces its own cause. The wisdom we seek is nothing but the result of our abortive attempts to discover wisdom. Follies are not stages on the road to wisdom; wisdom is essentially a form of folly.

ESPRIT D'ESCALIER

Factum stultus cognoscit

The principle of the retroactive effect rules the world. We must fail in order to gain the knowledge that allows us to understand our failures. Experience always comes too late, *post festum*. All wisdom is wisdom after the event, *esprit d'escalier*. During a banquet we search vainly for the cutting reply to an impertinent question; only as we go down the stairs does the right retort occur to us. Hence *l'esprit d'escalier*, the spirit at work in the giddying stairwell of our constructions, the sanctified space of wisdom in hindsight.

A fitting monument to the retroactive nature of our existence can be found in Kampen, the Dutch city inhabited by fools. Its citizens built a church but forgot the stairs to the tower, which is why an external staircase had to be added later.

EPIMETHEUS

Life can only be grasped by looking backwards,
But must be lived forwards.
Kierkegaard

I call all knowledge acquired after the event, all results obtained unintentionally, epimethean, in honour of the Titan Epimetheus ('afterthinker'), twin brother of Prometheus ('forethinker').

Epimetheus was charged with endowing every creature on Earth with the qualities it needed to survive. Thus he gave one animal strength without speed, and another speed without strength. Some he equipped with sharp claws, others with the safety of wings. In short, he created a natural balance in which no species would perish. But he forgot Man. (Had Prometheus had genuine foresight, he would have surely realized that Epimetheus would be remiss in the task assigned to him.)

To limit the damage, Prometheus stole Athene's intellect and Hephaistus' craftsmanship and gave them to Man. Hermes, for his part, provided the communal spirit. (See Plato, *Protagoras*, and Hesiod, *Theogony*)

Not Prometheus, but stupid Epimetheus, who 'grew wise through his mistakes', is the forefather of our civilization. His negligence forced mankind to embrace discipline and promote development. Our culture is simply the result of repeated attempts at belated damage containment. Wisdom flourishes against the grain. Failure is an undervalued phenomenon, although in statistical terms it is the most powerful factor of our existence.

Viewed in the light of *esprit d'escalier,* even the allegorical representation of *Prudentia* in the stairwell of the Amsterdam Theatre Institute takes on a new meaning. The great adversary of Stultitia is depicted holding the Mirror of Reflection and the Serpent of Circumspection.

PRODUCTIVE DELUSION

Epimethean causality can also be detected in the evasive manoeuvre leading the tragic hero to his prophesied doom. The idiotic, completely unfounded, prophecy owes its success to the hero's vain attempts to refute it.

Hamartia, blindness, is productive. The prophecy is self-fulfilling thanks to the hero's irrational fear of, or stubborn belief in, fictitious events that will only occur because they are expected. The imagined effect elicits a tangible cause. The prophecy of the outcome leads to the outcome of the prophecy. Without prediction there can be no grievous error, and without error no prophecy. Every prediction is epimethean in character; only after the event does a simple assertion become a genuine prophecy.

STUPIDITY AS THE MYSTICAL FOUNDATION OF OUR EXISTENCE

A fine kind of justice that is bounded by a river!
Truth on this side of the Pyrénées, error on the other.
Pascal, *Pensées*

We have blind faith in our knowledge, not because knowledge is wise or true by nature; it is considered wise and true simply because it is shared by the majority. We do not follow a rule because it is functional; a rule becomes functional once everybody follows it. We do not stop at traffic lights because the red colour forces us to stop. The red light has a regulating effect because we stop for it. In short, a rule owes its force not to arguments, but to the herd instinct. Not reason, but custom and habit govern our life.

Every new start is hilarious. Smilingly, we obey an initially idiotic rule, until it actually becomes functional, until there is good argument for it. In short, the effect precedes the cause: what we have here is a case of epimethean causality. Efficiency is not a natural aspect of rules and regulations, but the result of our compliance.

THE AUTOMATON

We are automata no less than men of intellect.
Pascal, *Pensées*

Though arguments may convince us of the wisdom of a rule, or indeed of its stupidity, the automaton inherent in man is governed by the force of habit, something that is more compelling than all the arguments for and against combined. Hence stupidity is not a matter of poor insight or poor knowledge, but of automatic responses.

LABORA, ASELLE, QUOMODO EGO
LABORAVI, ET PRODERIT TIBI

'Toil on, ass, as I have toiled, and it will stand you in
good stead.'
Graffito on the wall of a school on the Palatine Hill in
Rome (*c.* first century AD)

Though we know better, we put up with senseless ritual. Habit accustoms us to stupid rules until in the end we come to believe in them. Our conversion is only a matter of time.

No one can be converted to a stupid rule by argument. Argument only convinces those who are already 'steeped in stupidity', who consider all stupid rules the last word in wisdom. Anyone who claims that he does not follow a rule for its own sake, but because his reason tells him that it is fitting, simply fools himself. Argument is rationalization after the event; thought is epimethean by nature.

THE CREDO OF STUPIDITY

We obey the law, not because it is just, but because it is the law. The tautology reflects the unlawful basis of the law: the law is deemed just as soon a everyone obeys it. This idiotic aspect of the law seems to be an obstacle in its path, but is in fact its mystical justification. The constitutional state only exists by virtue of abortive attempts by citizens to live up to the demands of the law. It is just because the law always contains an incomprehensible element that it maintains its grip on us.

We do not have faith on reasonable grounds. We have faith because it is absurd, or rather, as Tertullian puts it: *quia ineptum est* and *quia impossibile est*, because it is silly and impossible. The same idiocy that prevents the marriage of behaviour and conviction is a prerequisite of religious faith. Faith flies in the face of knowledge. (Henning Schroër, *Die Denkform der Paradoxalität als theologisches Problem*, Göttingen, 1960)

THE REVERSAL

A river divides wisdom from stupidity; local customs and habits determine what is lawful and what is not. Unreflective action justifies rules and regulations in retrospect. This is because the idiotic basis of our social behaviour must remain hidden from us lest our regulations lose their power. Stupidity only works when it goes unrecognized. That is why we put the cart before the horse and act as if the law were naturally just. That is the role of the imagination.

THE INVISIBLE TREASURE

A rich farmer who felt death approaching said to his lazy sons: 'Be sure you do not sell my land because there is great treasure buried in it, although I do not know where.' When he died, the sons diligently ploughed up all the land in a vain search for the hidden treasure. But because of the ploughing that year's harvest earned them a fortune.

Retrospectively, their ploughing produced the treasure that made them plough. This fable by La Fontaine shows how imagination can be turned into reality, how imaginary treasure can give rise to real treasure. What is more, the farm would have had no future without their imagination. For had the idiocy of ploughing the land for the sake of ploughing been revealed to the sons, it would have been fatal to their morale.

That this is more than a fable is illustrated by a legal example.

THE JUDGE JUDGED

Fiat stultitia, pereat mundus
Let stupidity be done, though the world perish.

The judge acts as if he were teaching criminals a lesson. Yet research has shown that criminals rarely, if ever, reform. Strictly speaking, a judge passes sentence in order to maintain his own sense of justice and that of the citizens he represents. Yet the revelation that the judge is there to teach himself lessons would be disastrous for the legal system. That is the reason why we act as though the judge is there to educate the criminal.

All our organizations work by virtue of stupidity. Our world revolves round fantasies and around fools who believe in them. Stupidity is useful.

'KANNITVERSTAN'

Fruitful misunderstandings also play a large part in fostering morality, as witness Johann Peter Hebel's short story 'Kannitverstan' (*kan niet verstaan*, 'I can't understand') in the *Schatzkästlein des rheinischen Hausfreundes* (1811):

> 'If he feels so inclined, a man can ponder the inconstancy
> of all earthly things in Emmendingen and Gundelfingen,
> no less than in Amsterdam, and be reconciled to his lot,
> even though few windfalls come his way. Yet it was by the
> most extraordinarily roundabout route that a German
> journeyman in Amsterdam was led *by error to the truth*
> and to its understanding.'

The itinerant journeyman came upon a wonderful house 'filled with tulips, asters and night-scented stock'. He asked a passer-by in German for the name of the owner, to which the Dutchman replied 'Kannitverstan'.

In the harbour he saw a ship laden with precious cargo. When he asked about its owner, he was told once again 'Kannitverstan'.

Finally he saw a funeral procession and asked for the name of the deceased. 'Kannitverstan,' he was informed.

> 'Poor Kannitverstan,' he exclaimed. 'What good are all
> your riches to you now? No more than what I can look
> forward to in all my poverty: a sheet and a shroud, and of
> all your lovely flowers, perhaps a sprig of rosemary on
> your cold breast, or of rue.'

And if he ever again felt angry at the unfair distribution of the world's riches, he thought of Mr Kannitverstan in Amsterdam, of his grand house, his richly laden ship, his narrow grave, and was reconciled to his own lot.

BLESSED ARE THE POOR IN SPIRIT

It is (wrongly) said that the Jesuits act on the principle that the end justifies the means. The rule according to which we live, by contrast, is that the end is to justify our means, that is, all the rules and the order they entail, provided their idiocy is not understood. This reversal in the relation between end and means must remain hidden, because if it were known it would put an end to the bliss we derive from our Boeotian behaviour.

The bliss vanishes as soon as we realize that the unfathomable authority of the law does not exist except in our vain attempts to do justice to the law. Ignorance and bliss are closely linked: blessed are the poor in spirit. It's a pity that we are too stupid to realize this fact, though that realization would put an end to our bliss. But we can take pleasure in our displeasure . . .

LA BOÉTIE AND BOEOTIANA

What monstrous vice is it that does not even merit being called cowardice? Who can come up with a term vile enough for an evil that nature disowns and language refuses to name?

Etienne de la Boétie, *Discours de la servitude volontaire* (c. 1550)

1. Peasants collect water with a sieve.

2. The auctioneer sings the praises of the peasant's worthless cow so enthusiastically that the peasant pays a fortune to buy the beast back.

3. A peasant on skates races his own shadow, which he has taken for another skater.

4. A peasant fools everyone into believing that a whale has been stranded. When they all rush to the beach, he starts to believe his own story and races after them.

5. A peasant sells a cock and four hens to a passer-by. The buyer has no money on him, so the peasant accepts the cock as a pledge.

These five Boeotiana are not reversals of the norm but portray aberrations at work in normalcy itself. By way of illustration, I shall compare them with pronouncements by La Boétie in his *Discours*. His analysis of power covers five aspects of stupidity: the force of habit; its side effect; the link between fascination and ignorance; imagination and bliss.

1. 'Habit teaches us to submit and to swallow the poison of slavery without finding it bitter – legend has it that Mithridates made a habit of drinking poison.'

2. We are not the tyrant's victims; the tyrant owes his power to us. 'What could he do to us if we ceased to act as receivers for the thief who robs us, accomplices of the murderer who slays us and traitors to our better selves?'

3. The tyrant does not owe his authority to some extraordinary powers; precisely the opposite is true: the tyrant exercises his power only while his 'idiotic' nature remains hidden. 'The kings of Assyria appeared before the people as rarely as possible, lest the people began to wonder whether their kings might be nothing more than ordinary men. [...] The king's mysterious nature thus helped to accustom his people to their slavery, and caused them to serve him all the more readily in that they did not know their master and could not even tell, except with the greatest difficulty, whether they had a master in the first place; all went in fear of someone nobody had ever seen.'

4. 'The common people believed that Pyrrhus' big toe could perform miracles and cure diseases of the spleen.' We are not the victims of the tyrant's magical powers but 'the people themselves dream up the figments of the imagination in which they eventually come to believe.'

5. If his subjects should only want to do so, they could easily put an end to the tyrant's power. Why then do they willingly remain slaves? Because they, too, profit from their slavery. They believe that the tyrant shares his riches with them, when in fact it is the other way round: 'The fools fail to realize that they have

received no more than a small portion of what is really theirs.'

But there is yet another reason. 'Mankind spurns freedom.' Why is that? 'Because it can be acquired far too easily.' Here lies the 'evil that language refuses to name', the crux of stupidity: we take secret comfort in discomfort. And we find bliss in the masochism to which all stupidities bear witness. After every disaster, the fools fling themselves wantonly into the next task doomed to failure.

GOTHAMITE WISDOM

Stupidity is not so much rooted in error; it is persistence in error, often against better judgement. Even thought patterns that begin by helping man on his way will turn against him in the long run – a reversal that hinges on his stupidity.

According to Henri Bergson, repetition, reversal and misunderstanding are the three tricks employed by farce to expose this stupid, mechanical form of behaviour (in *Le Rire*, 1900; trans. as *Laughter*, 1911). However, the blind automatism that, according to Bergson, puts obstacles in the way of evolution, is, in fact, the motor that keeps the world turning. We do not laugh in order to correct this rigid, mechanical, unconscious form of behaviour, as Bergson thought we do, but because we are playing games with a truth that is taboo. Gothamite jokes impinge on the idiocy constituting the mystical foundation of our civilization. Such jokes provide comical illustrations of the tragic crux of our existence, of the fact that men grow wise through adversity. Disasters are the matrix of human success.

People who risk their lives are comical, not because their actions are unreasonable, but because they expose the folly on which reason is founded. We laugh nervously at puppets mimicking what we do unwittingly. Our laughter bears witness to our uneasy conscience.

Jokes are weapons in the fight against stupor. On the one hand they keep the idea of the idiotic core of our existence alive; this prevents delusion. On the other hand they elicit a slight sense of panic, which helps to purge us of the fear of stupidity; this saves us from utter bewilderment.

Woodcut of men
raising beams, from
Das Schiltbürgerbuch
(1680)

THE LOGIC OF DUAL STUPIDITY

Some fools decide to build a municipal hall. To that end they go to the top of a mountain and begin felling the required trees. Next they carry the logs down. In the process, one log accidentally slips out of their hands and rolls down the rest of the way. That gives them an idea: it is obviously more sensible to roll the logs down the mountain. So they pick up all those they have already brought down, carry them back to the top of the mountain and then roll them down to the bottom.

The two contradictory operations illustrate the logic of the two stupid actions. The first is carrying the logs down the mountain. In a sense this is a useful stupidity, as sound as reason itself; it constitutes a part of the thought process, of the cycle of rising and falling. This stupidity is responsible for the adversity by which we grow 'wise'. It produces the scars that jointly form our character.

The second type of stupidity is found in the reverse operation: the logs are manhandled back up the mountain. This stupidity explodes the thought process, for what we have here is not stupidity in thinking but the stupidity *of* thinking.

Understanding the first type of stupidity leads to insight, is evolutionary, contributes to our development. Seeing through the stupidity of thinking on the other hand is revolutionary. Its consequence is madness or redemption: thought is liberated from its confining laws and the road thrown open to the creation of new forms of thought *ex nihilo*.

These two types of stupidity are also found in the Stoic concept of *stultitia*, meaning both stupidity and madness. Thinking is a game in which we can lose or win some knowledge, but we can also lose the game itself.

THE COMIC HIATUS

In the classic cartoon scene, Bugs Bunny runs over the edge of the precipice. He walks through the air for a few moments, with no ground beneath his feet. Only when he looks down and takes stock of his situation – 'uh, oh' – does he start to fall. In my humble opinion, all mankind is to be found in this comic hiatus. Our existence is confined to the realm between *stupidity that is by definition unrecognized and the disastrous comprehension of our stupidity*.

No one is intelligent enough to comprehend his own stupidity. And that is all to the good. Cognition has a disastrous effect not only on stupidity, but also on the intelligence based on it.

Anyone who behaves stupidly fails to see that he is stupid, and will persist in his folly. In a sense, he is still intelligent, that is, he continues to think while he pursues the false trail he has taken.

Awareness of one's stupidity not only means putting an end to that stupidity but also to the knowledge based on it. Insight coincides with idiocy.

THE SEVENTH HEAVEN

This realm between the two types of stupidity, between stupidity and the idiocy springing from comprehension, is the domain of the comic effect. In the animated cartoon, heroes explode, are smashed to a pulp or skinned alive, only to get up again as if nothing has happened. And even the Irish in Irish jokes go on coming to grief without Ireland going under.

Man does not differ from the cardboard figures in animated cartoons. We too keep falling flat on our faces and standing up again merrily, as if some intelligence guarantees not only that we survive all foolish acts, but also that we learn from our mistakes. Gullibly we dwell in a paradisiacal state, in which intelligence thinks for us. Our blind faith in reason lends all our actions a comical, unreal, indestructible aspect, in short, something typically Irish.

From Margit Willems and P. Hermanides,
Speciale effecten (Amsterdam, 1991)

THE SECRET OF SUSPENDED LIFE

Our life is in a state of suspension. Every man goes on thinking and talking in the void, stumbling about in the illusory coordinates of his knowledge, trusting blindly in the rational basis of his existence, much as trapeze artists trust in their safety net. Like the rabbit that walks on air.

Why doesn't the rabbit fall down? Because it is in an animated cartoon. But let us adopt the logic of the cartoon for a moment: the rabbit continues to remain suspended in the air because the force of gravity has been temporarily switched off, because nature has forgotten its own laws. Things are much the same in fairy-tales: even the most fearsome giants would end up with crippled backs the moment gravity is brought into play. (This leads one to suspect that fairy stories about giants are written by people with sore backs.)

The secret of the joke is revealed in Friz Freleng's animated cartoon *High Diving Hare* (1949). Cowboy Yosemite Sam goes to a circus that advertises a death-defying leap: a dive from the top of the circus tent

47

Bugs Bunny in *High Diving Hare*. From Joe Adamson, *Bugs Bunny*, (London, 1991)

into a tub of water. It turns out that the artiste is indisposed, so Sam forces the ringmaster, Bugs Bunny, to stand in for him. Trussed up with rope, Bugs is poised on the diving board that is attached to a platform on top of a ladder. Sam, perched on the platform, saws the board off: immediately stupid Sam goes crashing down, platform and ladder and all, while clever Bugs Bunny remains suspended in the air on the sawn-off diving board and tells the audience: 'I know dis defies de law of gravity, but, uh, you see, I never studied law!' As if gravity only works if we are familiar with its effects. The joke is that the rabbit knows perfectly well that there is something he does not know. And as long as he does not know it he is safe.

THE STUPIDITY OF INTELLIGENCE

Everybody knows that our knowledge is unfounded, that science is a self-defined system of rules and laws. And as long as we all act dumb and pretend that our wisdom is soundly based, everything goes without a hitch. Imagination keeps the world going round. Disclosure of the obvious, however, would prove fatal.

But whom are we fooling? If everyone knows at the back of his mind that our knowledge is baseless, who can there be who does not know this? Who persists in flying in the face of all the evidence and continues to believe in the solid basis of our knowledge? The paradoxical answer is: our intelligence does not and cannot know it. Thinking has an inbuilt safety mechanism; our thought patterns prevent us from directly recognizing stupidity. Intelligence stops us from taking cognizance of stupidity. No man is intelligent enough to grasp his own stupidity, and even that fact passes all human understanding.

The stupidity of our intelligence is that we cannot recognize its stupidity. However, that inability also reflects the hidden wisdom of our intelligence. The discovery that all our knowledge is built on stupidity would deprive us of knowledge, undermine its legitimacy, and invalidate this very insight, which, after all, rests on our knowledge.

THE RICHES OF SPIJK

Stupidity is twice your lot:
An ignoramus, you, my friend! And yet, you know it not!
Jeremias de Decker

The entrance and the exit to rationality are both blocked by a classical paradox: *Learning cannot be learned* and *Thought cannot be unthought* (which misled philosophers into a very human stupidity: 'I think that I think', and to a divine inanity: 'I am who I am'.)

At the gates of stupidity, too, we come upon two perplexing monsters. On the one hand: *stupidity is unattainable*. Nobody can become stupid. Thought undermines the intention of the would-be fool. Every act, however stupid, betrays its underlying reason. But even his intention plays the would-be fool false. You cannot prove that you are stupid by deliberately acting the fool.

On the other hand: *stupidity cannot be avoided*. The fool cannot simply say: 'No fooling, let's get serious.' Even if he did, his intelligence would already have the status of stupidity.

How then can we gain an understanding of stupidity? Anyone who is stupid cannot know what stupidity is – and not even that. Anyone not stupid does not know what it is to be stupid.

Not only ignorance, but knowledge, too, plays us tricks. Our thinking cannot dispense with the commonplaces that stand in the way of genuine wisdom. The contrast between stupidity and intelligence is itself another commonplace preventing us from identifying stupidity. The stupidity of our understanding bars our understanding of stupidity.

Conversely, growing understanding takes us further and further away from the stupidity we try to grasp. Knowledge of stupidity impairs our view of the stupidity of knowledge.

In short, stupidity is unattainable, yet cannot be avoided, and that is the dilemma of the morosopher. We are stuck with our cocksureness. The situation is as hopeless as that of the northern Dutch village of Spijk, built with streets all higgledy piggledy around a church. Visitors who fail to pay attention invariably miss the exit. The story has it that a farm worker from Westphalia, trying to leave the village, walked 36 times round the church and exclaimed in amazement: 'What a rich place Spijk is! It must have at least 36 smithies!'

We deem ourselves rich in wisdom in much the same way.

SOWING SALT

A good encyclopædia contains nothing original.
Lorenzo Morales, *Morosofia* (1597)

How can we demonstrate the stupidity of our intelligence if in order to do so we have to rely on that very intelligence? With the help of a patently foolish theory. Only by using a system that betrays its own stupidity can we avoid the snares of the wiseacre.

The starting point is: *I am stupid!* With that statement we join the ranks of a long history of authors who have written about foolishness. Either the statement is wise, in which case it is its own refutation; or else it is stupid, in which case it testifies to the wisdom of the statement. In short, the impossible premise keeps the gulf between wisdom and stupidity open, the gap that keeps thought alive. The premise obeys the Megarian logic of the liar's paradox. Megara was a city in ancient Greece famous not only for its stupidity but also for its academy, which specialized in being eristic, the art of being in the right even when one is in the wrong. The structure of fallacies and the rules of comedy are intimately related. The method we are adopting here, by contrast, is no parody, no caricature of thought, but a faithful imitation of the folly at work in our minds.

We plagiarize and combine figures of thought to strip them of their petrifying effect and to highlight their bewildering obverse. Both aspects are enshrined in the word 'stupor', etymologically related to 'stupidity'. It is not to wisdom that we should look for a cure of stupidity, but to the dialectic inherent in stupidity itself.

The eristic stance provides the instruments needed for laying bare the stupid but efficient strategies by which we come to grips with our existence. 'Stupid', because these strategies only work when unrecognized. That is also true of lies, but unlike the liar, the fool is deaf to his own rhetoric.

We do not oppose this self-deception with a philosophical or logical truth, but with a rhetorical, paralogical truth. Through the form, we try to transcend the dubious content. Our efforts aim to arrive at an unfounded theory that renders stupidity tangible, and at the same time, indirectly, in a playful way, points to an alternative. The moral lies in the method: by imitating stupidity we render wisdom productive.

We plough the sand, sow the salt, and harvest sea holly.

LODGED IN STUPIDITY

Potius deficere quam desperare
Better to fail than to despair
Motto of the Amsterdam Lyceum

A building in the centre of Amsterdam, long since demolished, once housed the Stupidity Hotel. When its manager still worked as a chambermaid in the Carlton Hotel round the corner, she once expressed her desire to go into business for herself someday. But people told her she was too stupid for that. With no way of escaping her reputation, she lodged in her own stupidity and exploited it.

METHODICAL STUPIDITY

On the basis of a folly repeated having the force of truth (*bis stultitia veritatem valet*), it has been said that wisdom is nothing but the remembrance of past mistakes.
M. Psittacus, in Max Jacob, *Le Phanérogame* (1907)

Stupidity is a taboo. There is good reason why we laugh at the stupidity of others and try with all our might to hide our own. But how to live with our stupidity? How can we stop being victims of our own folly?

The struggle against stupidity is pointless. Intelligence attacking stupidity becomes caught in its own web of thought patterns. Prevention is useless. Anyone acting stupidly notices it, by definition, too late. A stupid act cannot be headed off. The most stupid solution is to be struck dumb by the fear of doing something stupid.

The best cure for a stupid action is to repeat it at once. Repetition draws the tragic sting from the stupid act, turns stupidity into a joke. Unconscious stupidity becomes conscious stupidity; people readily mistake you for a humorist – in our society the very epitome of wit.

Methodical stupidity can be exemplified by two related stories. When a South African visitor to The Netherlands, unfamiliar with Dutch court etiquette, drank up all the water in his fingerbowl, Queen Wilhelmina courteously did the same. The repetition drew the sting from the visitor's stupidity.

The second story concerns a Chinese visitor in Africa, who was served a banana and, unfamiliar with the fruit, ate it, peel and all. To teach the visitor a lesson, his discourteous host demonstratively peeled his own banana. The visitor watched, then took another banana and again ate it peel and all, declaring that, in his view, it tasted better like that. Once more, the repetition drew the sting from a stupid act.

Stupidity is unavoidable. Make your stupidity a personal, unique stupidity. If you fail, fail at the highest possible level. If you fall, fall with elegance and a song in your heart. Be as colourfully and versatilely stupid as you can. That way you avoid blandness and rigidity, the two dangerous sides of stupidity. Make stupidity your most redeeming quality.

THREE

Fallor, the Aerobat

Stupidity is not my strong point.
Paul Valéry, *Monsieur Teste* (1895)

CREDO

No one is intelligent enough to understand his own stupidity. And that is all to the good. Our vain attempts to come to grips with our own stupidity jointly constitute our intelligence. 'Every time I think I am stupid, I confirm my self.'

WHO IS FALLOR?

Fallor differs in language, dress and eating habits from his friends and enemies. These differences define his being. In short, his identity is guaranteed by an outer boundary.

But Fallor also has an inner boundary, for when is he the real Fallor? Strictly speaking, never. Fallor believes he knows himself with all his good and bad points, but he is always being struck dumb by his own idiocy.

The real Fallor does not exist, but that's no problem. Fallor is Fallor only in his more or less colourful, but vain, attempts to prove himself. Stupidity is his forte. Failure defines his identity. 'And if failure is inevitable, then preferably at the highest level.'

Fallor developed these ideas while he was pedalling away on his home-trainer, the only place where, every now and then, he reached his limits.

A FEAST FOR PESSIMISTS

Fallor does not live his life because it is particularly true, good, or beautiful, but because life happens to be what it is, that is, idiotic. Because this realization is too much – or too little – for him, he acts either as if life were true, good and beautiful, or as if it were mendacious, bad and ugly. Life is a real feast for pessimists: everything turns out better than expected.

THE EARLOBE

It is an old Jewish custom to lay one brick askew in a new building, as a token of man's imperfection. Persians deliberately weave a flaw into their carpets because they do not wish to compete with God's infallibility. After Fallor's birth, his mother bit a small piece out of his earlobe.

These humble acts bear witness to hubris, but as such they are the evidence of imperfection . . .

PERSONAL COLUMN

While playing with wife, young father jumps over the laid dinner table and crushes infant.

TOWARDS AN AESTHETICS OF STUPIDITY

With his suitcase, Fallor pushed the glass doors of the Porta Cornea Hotel open. As if testing the weary guests, the motto *Per non dormire* had been inscribed beneath the stained-glass poppies. Sleeping by not sleeping . . . Befuddled by this dialectic, Fallor dropped onto the bed in his room.

Something was still wrong. After a few minutes it dawned on Fallor that the abstract motifs on the wallpaper entirely lacked either pattern or symmetry.

In his *Critique of Judgment*, Immanuel Kant mentions three examples of pure beauty: military marches, hummingbirds, and wallpaper patterns. Purposiveness without purpose, provided it leads to a harmony of understanding and imagination, guarantees a disinterested satisfaction.

The chaotic design on the walls and the ceiling of his hotel room, by contrast, gave Fallor a feeling of unease because it was quite beyond his comprehension and imagination.

By imagining that the wallpaper in the adjoining room was a faithful mirror image of the wallpaper in his own, he might perhaps have ensured himself a good night's sleep. However, Fallor resisted the temptation to invent some Great Paperhanger. He preferred to welcome the disquieting design as an aid to self-realization. Fallor became Fallor in the vain struggle with the elements that kept him from finding himself. ·

Self-assured, he fell into a deep sleep.

FURTHER CONTRIBUTIONS TO THE AESTHETICS OF STUPIDITY

The next morning, Fallor cycled on the spot for some twenty kilometres with a clear view of the mirror above his washbasin. A little later he lost himself in some new aerobatic feats.

Wars, stellar systems and the dome of St Peter's in Rome arouse displeasure because they are beyond our imagination. Yet precisely by emphasizing our inadequacy, they provide an indirect foretaste of a Higher Power, which, according to Kant, creates pleasure in displeasure.

Megaric logic, by contrast, led Fallor to the assumption that the Sublime is defined by our folly. The supersensory sphere exists solely thanks to our bewilderment. 'The unchained elements sing of the stupidity of man.'

Through this mental leap, Fallor came to himself. He folded his exercise bike, put it in its travelling case and left the Porta Eburnea Hotel.

HOMEOPATHIC STUPIDITY

To temper the tragedy of his slip-ups, Fallor invariably added a drop of stupidity to his actions. Not that he deliberately did foolish things. By definition, stupidity works only unseen and undesired. But how to proceed? The drop of stupidity is the Utopian, absurd, impossible element characteristic of every well-chosen objective; something that is doomed to failure, and only then leads us on to wisdom through adversity.

FROM THE SUBLIME TO THE RIDICULOUS

Fallor's back garden was crammed with gigantic sculptures, home-made attempts to give some shape to his life: a device made up of saucepans, feathers and bunting, a never-ending ha-ha, a monumental obelisk and other ambitious constructions.

Strictly speaking, the sculptural works were sublime failures. None could possibly convey an adequate idea of Fallor's life. But through their failure, the sculptures gave an indirect hint of what his life might have been. They succeeded in their very lack of success. Full of himself, Fallor would stand in the garden for days.

The neighbours often wondered if he would be able to carry on without his sculptures. Did Fallor have any kind of life outside these hopeless attempts to come to grips with his existence?

No problem. To Fallor the sublime was ridiculous; in their enormity the sculptures were tangible expressions of the lack of success that his life in essence was. Slowly, the device with the saucepans, feathers and bunting would jerk into motion, to cheer Fallor's failure.

THE UNHEARD-OF STUDY

Every other day Fallor ate in the *Tête-à-queue* restaurant. The regulars were served at long tables. Fallor took a seat next to them. 'What right have you got to sit here?' asked his neighbour. With genuine interest, Fallor enquired if the man might be studying law.

'Guess again,' said the student.
'Leisure studies? Town planning? Ergonomics?'
The man looked at him and smiled.
'Psychology? Anthroposophy? Philosophy?'

Fallor was doing his level best to guess correctly. 'Economics? Astronomy? Architecture?' Amused, the student encouraged him to go on. Fallor named all the subjects he could think of. 'Literature? Archaeology? Musicology?' Gradually the smile left the student's face. 'Mathematics? Medicine? Science?' Fallor's doubt grew in direct proportion to his neighbour's. Who was pulling whose leg?

When Fallor began to repeat himself because he could think of no more new subjects, his neighbour became convinced that Fallor was well aware of exactly what subject he was studying.

Exasperated, the student walked out. The man of successful failures had struck again.

MOROLOGY

There is no such thing as applied morology. The laws of stupidity cannot be translated into practice. Any attempt to cause a failure for the sake of the profitable side effect is self-defeating. The laws of morology only work when applied unwittingly.

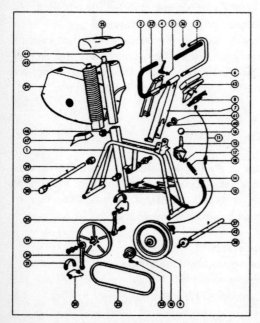

Exploded diagram of
Fallor's secret weapon: the
GULF Home Trainer.

It is very much like Murphy's Law: 'If something can go wrong it will.' But do not try to apply that law, for if you do you will fall victim to Silberman's Paradox: 'If Murphy's Law can go wrong, it will.' (Arthur Bloch, *Murphy's Law: All the Reasons Why Everything Goes Wrong*, London, 1985)

Even so, Fallor took lessons in stumbling at the drama school, and his futile attempts at falling over were a roaring success.

FALLOR ON HOLIDAY

On the way, Mr Fallor stopped to wait until the river had passed.

FOUR

The Ha-Ha

THREE STUPID MAPS

If we want to draw an accurate map of the world, then we must also include the map itself in that map, which in turn must include a map of the map of the map, and so on *ad infinitum*. The paradox of the embedded map was described in 1899 by Josiah Royce in his *The World and the Individual*.

An entirely different type of infinity is found in the paradox of the perfect map described in *Sylvie and Bruno Concluded* (1893) by Lewis Carroll. A character called Mein Herr tells of a map that was continuously being perfected and enlarged until it reached the scale of 'one mile to the mile'. However the farmers objected; they were afraid that the map, once unfolded, would cover the whole country and shut out the sunlight.

In the end, someone thought of using the country itself as its own map; and the country has been playing that role for its inhabitants ever since.

The three types of map illustrate the problem of stupidity. All order is beset with a totalitarian temptation. However, the quest for wholeness is undermined by a form of idiocy on which every type of organization founders sooner or later, an intangible madness that threatens to turn the whole system into a farce. Infinite regression also teaches us that ultimately it is the map itself that stands in the way of our successful mapping of the world.

Idiocy poses a threat to order; the attempt to come to direct grips with idiocy would lead to bewilderment. At the same time, however, none of our constructions would work in the complete absence of idiocy: idiocy prevents delusion. Idiocy makes one think.

Bewilderment and delusion are two forms of stupor. Too much idiocy leads to panic; too little idiocy to stupefaction, as the paradox of the perfect map makes clear. In short, we must keep idiocy at bay even while embracing it.

And that brings us to the question of whether it is possible to produce a perfect map of the world. The reason why all attempts have failed is that the map can only be drawn if failure is taken as our starting-point. Only an order that keeps reminding us that it is unattainable prevents panic and its obverse here, delusion. Hence the best solution is to use the world as its own map, for only in that way is the foolishness of the entire enterprise made manifest.

There is nevertheless the danger that, in the long run, we overlook the inherent foolishness, the empty space separating the world from itself as its own map, and hence come to believe that everything is self-evident. To understand this point, we have to look at the role of the ha-ha in French and English landscape design.

THE FOOLISHNESS OF THE FRENCH GARDEN

'Le Nôtre enclosed boredom within his walls.'
Marquis de Lezay-Marnésia, *Les Paysages* (1800)

The most important representative of French landscape architecture was André Le Nôtre (1613–1700). In 1640 this mathematician, draughtsman and horticulturalist was appointed landscape gardener at Versailles by Louis XIV. Applying the geometrical laws of linear perspective, he declared war on nature.

The formal French garden at Versailles is built round a central axis that runs in a straight line from the château to the horizon, with on either side symmetrically placed open parterres, fountains, symbolic statues, and ornamental basins reflecting the sky. From the staircase fronting the chateau, the visitor can take in the entire spectacle at a glance. Reflecting the motto of Louis XIV, *Ut vidi, vici*, the garden is captured the moment you see it. That is also its main disadvantage: the French garden leaves nothing to the imagination. The symmetry quickly palls:

> . . . *La nature féconde*
> *Varie à chaque instant le théâtre du monde;*

Et nous, dans nos enclos stérilement ornés,
Nous la bornons sans cesse à nos desseins bornés:
Là, j'admire un moment l'ordre, la symétrie;
Et ce plaisir d'un jour est l'ennui de la vie.

. . . Fertile nature
Changes the world stage hour by hour;
And we, within our barrenly ornate confines,
Ever restrict her to our restricting designs:
For a moment I marvel at the order, the symmetry;
Then that brief pleasure becomes a lifelong ennui.

Saint-Lambert, *Les Saisons* (1785)

While the symmetry within the garden may be too much of a good thing, there is a flaw awaiting us at its outer edge, for no matter how extensive a monarch's estate, sooner or later we are bound to come up against a wall. Such a wall gives us an alarming feeling of immurement. Moreover, it arouses a secret desire to discover what lies beyond. We suspect still finer vistas lie on the other side. This disquiet spoils our enjoyment of the garden.

The wall not only divides culture from the surrounding nature, it also brings home to us the inherent limitations of the formal garden, its fundamental insularity, which is all the more obvious when materialized by a wall. The symmetry has an oppressive effect. We feel out of place, banished from nature unconfined. In order to shake off this malaise, many French gardens include an ah-ah.

THE AH-AH!

The taste for views and distant prospects springs from the inclination of most men to seek pleasure where they do not happen to be.

Jean-Jacques Rousseau, *La nouvelle Héloïse* (1761)

A definition of the ah-ah can be found in Diderot and d'Alembert's *Encyclopédie* (vol. 1, 1751) in the article 'Ah!-Ah!' contributed by A.-J. Dézallier d'Argenville:

An ah-ah at Versailles

AH-AH (Garden Design), *claire voie or sault de loupe.* These words refer to an opening in a wall, but without a gate, at the same height as the avenues, with a ditch at its base that catches us by surprise and elicits an 'ah-ah!' It is alleged that Monseigneur, the son of Louis xiv, coined this term when he was walking in the gardens of Meudon.

In several places the walls around Meudon's garden have been replaced with deep trenches, which cannot be seen from a distance. In fact, the ah-ah is of military origin, and was meant to serve as a trap for enemy cavalry. In landscape design, however, the ah-ah rids us of the sense of being hemmed in by affording us an unimpeded view of the countryside. At the same time it keeps intruders out. Yet not even the ah-ah can reconcile us to the garden – on the contrary. The eye strays into the distance rather than remain confined to what is close at hand. Paradise is elsewhere. Only a poor artist, who cannot satisfy us with our immediate surroundings, has to resort to distant views. The ah-ah bears witness to an artistic failure and at the same time causes frustration. We see small segments of nature, when what we really want is to enjoy the full view, unhampered by obstacles. The discovery of the ditch makes us aware of the ridiculous aspect of the garden. 'Ah-ah!' is an exclamation not only of surprise, but also of disappointment.

In the gardens at Versailles, by contrast, the aim is to relieve the hemmed-in feeling by creating the illusion by means of ah-ahs that the garden encompasses the whole world. Unimpeded by walls, paths run from the central canal to the horizon, visual axes suggesting that nothing exists outside the garden. This apparently infinite layout symbolizes the unconfined powers of the sovereign.

But this absolutism, too, was doomed to failure; its sole effect was to make us perceive the confinement itself as unending. The world was turned into a prison without walls.

The discovery of the ah-ah put an end to the illusion of unbounded space, but also emphasized the foolishness of the layout. 'Ah-ah!' is an exclamation of surprise, and at the same time a sigh of relief.

French gardens are never felt to be second nature. Nowhere are they self-evident. How then are we to deal with the foolishness inherent in every garden? Easy. By turning the ah-ah into a ha-ha!

THE FOOLISHNESS OF THE ENGLISH GARDEN

The leading light of English landscape gardening was Lancelot Brown (1715–1783), nicknamed 'Capability' because he had the gift of sizing up the capabilities of a country estate quickly and skilfully. His ideal was an 'improved' version of the English countryside. In other words, we are confronted with an aesthetic tautology; his object was to transform nature into a garden resembling nature. The ideal English garden was a rural landscape.

A ride on horseback around a country estate and a few calculations were all Brown needed to draw up a plan. In the gardens of Hampton Court Palace he explained his method to Hannah More, using a striking metaphor:

> Now there he said (pointing a finger), I make a comma and,
> pointing to another spot where a more decided turn is proper,
> I make a colon; at another point (where an interruption is
> desirable to break the view) a parenthesis – now a full stop,
> and then I begin another subject.
>
> Hannah More to her sister, 31 December 1782

As if all he did was to discover the right punctuation marks the better to allow nature to speak for herself. But in fact the voice was Brown's own, at least according to William Cowper in his poem *The Task* (1785):

> He speaks. The lake in front becomes a lawn;
> Woods vanish, hills subside, and valleys rise;
> And streams, as if created for his use
> Pursue the track of his directing wand . . .

To attain his ideal, Brown literally moved mountains, shifted villages, dug lakes, drowned valleys, and had thousands of trees cut down or planted. When he spoke of the 'capabilities' of the land, it sounded like a parody of the *genius loci*, the spirit that, according to the Romans, dwells naturally in every landscape. The 'spirit' revealed by Brown, however, was more a retroactive effect of his apparently rash, but in fact visionary, interventions. He planned everything with an eye to future generations. He himself would never see the results. Timber posts would be needed for years to protect the stands of young saplings from cattle. And as the gardens reached full maturity, their artificial origins were gradually forgotten. Much of what we now think of as the characteristic natural landscape of the English lowlands is the work of Brown. On his death in 1783, Horace Walpole wrote:

> Such was the effect of his genius that when he was the happiest man, he will be least remembered; so closely did he copy nature that his works will be mistaken.

THE HA-HA

Prata rident
The meadows laugh.
Emanuele Tesauro, *Il cannocchiale aristotelico* (1654)

The trick facilitating the creation of the landscape garden and transforming the look of England so radically was the introduction of the ha-ha. According to Walpole, in his *History of the Modern Taste in Gardening* (1782),

64

the capital stroke, the leading step to all that has followed, was (I believe the thought was Bridgeman's) the destruction of walls for boundaries, and the invention of fosses – an attempt then deemed so astonishing, that the common people called them Ha! Ha!s, to express their surprise at finding a sudden and unperceived check to their walk.

Note that it was not the monarch who was astonished, but the common people. With the political landscape, the garden, too, changed its appearance. To create the illusion of a natural environment, walls had to make way for ditches. On the inner side of the ditch a special wall was built; on the other, the ground sloped up to the level of the land, so that livestock could graze there and keep the ditch free of weeds. In hilly country, a wall was erected and soil piled up against it. A drain was laid along the bottom.

Thanks to the ha-ha, distant fields give the impression of being a continuation of the garden, except that the sheep cannot cross into the garden.

The wand'ring flocks that browse between the shades,
Seem oft to pass their bounds; the dubious eye
Decides not if they crop the mead or lawn.
William Mason, *The English Garden* (1772–82)

Some ha-ha variants

Where the garden apparently passes seamlessly into the country-side, there lies a hidden ha-ha. It allows an uninterrupted view of the surrounding landscape. The garden 'blends' with the fields to form a splendid park.

SECOND NATURE

I greatly fear that nature herself is nothing but first habit, much as a habit is but second nature.

Pascal, *Pensées*

That first nature is already second nature is shown in caricature by the English garden. Thus Walpole said of the landscape gardener William Kent, Brown's mentor: 'He leaped the fence, and saw that all nature was a garden.' On that principle, the garden has been so far integrated into nature that it can no longer be recognized as such. That is the trick of naturalism. The English garden disappears into its own ideal: the garden becomes landscape, nature its own park. According to Rousseau, the complete absence of art guarantees the perfection of a garden, but what we have in England is a garden whose perfection is guaranteed by the absence of a garden.

It is a commonplace to say that our view of nature is culturally deter-mined. What should be added is that every self-evident piece of nature comprises a ha-ha.

Unlike in the French garden, the discovery of the ha-ha did not put an end to an illusion – the English garden could no longer be distin-guished from its surroundings. 'Ha-ha' is an exclamation of mild sur-prise. We laugh at the apparently pointless ditch. But our laughter dies on our lips the moment we realize that this element shapes the 'nature' in which we roam.

NATURE'S ORCHESTRA PIT

A true artist should put a generous deceit on the spectators.

Edmund Burke, *A Philosophical Enquiry into the Origins of Our Ideas of the Sublime and Beautiful* (1756)

In David Garrick's play *Lethe, or Esop in the Shades* (1740) we encounter Aesop on the banks of the Styx, accompanied by Lord Chalkstone, a champion of Capability Brown, who makes critical comments about the design of the underworld. In particular, he refers to the Elysian Fields:

> . . . which, by the way, Mr. Esop, are laid out most detestably –
> no taste! No fancy in the whole world! Your river there, what
> d'ye call it? Aye, Styx – why, 'tis as straight as Fleet-ditch. You
> should have given it a serpentine sweep, and sloped the banks
> of it. The place indeed has fine Capabilities; but you should
> clear the wood to the left, and the clump of trees to the right;
> in short, the whole wants variety, extent, contrast, inequality.
> (Going towards the Orchestra, stops suddenly, and looks into
> the Pit.) Upon my word, here's a fine Hah-hah!

The orchestra pit enhances the illusion created on the stage, provided only it is not noticed. Similarly, the ha-ha is the hidden point from which the English garden is conducted.

Just like the French ah-ah, the English ha-ha not only marks the formal division between garden and surrounding land, but also the limitations inherent in every garden. There is, however, a considerable difference between the two types of garden.

The boundary of the French garden is the garden itself: ultimately, the potentially pleasing form has a stifling effect. In a vain attempt to escape from this structural garden foolishness, the ah-ah grants us a glimpse of unspoilt nature, or the suggestion of infinite culture.

In the English landscape, by contrast, the stupidity inherent to gardens becomes a source of aesthetic pleasure. The garden is transformed from an area surrounded by walls into a park that is indistinguishable from nature and revolves around the ha-ha; in short, the boundary has became the pivotal point. The oppressive form is changed into a driving force. The English garden owes its dynamism

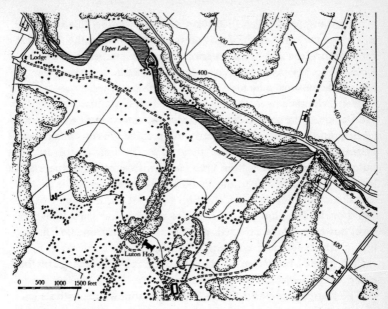

The ha-ha at Luton Hoo

to the inherent tension, not between culture and nature, but between 'nature', insofar as it is cultivated, and the unrestrained folly that has found a place within the confines of the ha-ha. The garden acquires a natural aspect in the series of vain attempts to turn it into a second nature. The English landscape is an inconstant garden, a contradiction in terms.

That is the trick on which Burke's aesthetics is based.

EROTIC EMPIRICISM

> Beauty in distress is much the most affecting beauty.
> Edmund Burke, *A Philosophical Enquiry*

Like their French colleagues, English landscape designers declared war on nature. Nature was considered to be a 'raw goddess', one that would never attain perfection without the divine reason of man, who selects what is best in nature and removes the 'flaws': 'Where nature failed, Brown acted.'

According to the Neo-Platonists, perfectly ordered Nature alone can reveal the spirit of the True and the Good through the Beautiful. From nature, the artist must develop forms that render the ideal 'tangible'. Hence the fallacy that man improves Nature so that he may in his turn be improved by the revealed 'Truth' of Nature.

Neo-Platonism holds the key to the gardens of William Kent, but in order to grasp the success of his disciple Brown, we must delve into the erotic empiricism of Edmund Burke as enshrined in his *Philosophical Enquiry into the Origin of Our Ideas of the Sublime and Beautiful*, published in 1756, around the time that Brown started his career as a landscape designer. According to Burke, nature's message is neither moralistic nor didactic. The Beautiful does not evoke the idea of the Good or the True, but of . . . Love! Not platonic, but sensual love. By love, however, Burke referred, not to lust or untrammelled desire, but to tenderness and affection. Gardens do not carry us to more exalted spheres, but reconcile us to life on earth by producing tangible evidence of their own imperfection.

The French garden is ruled by human reason, which, with its laws of dimensions and proportions, changes trees into pillars, pyramids and obelisks, hedges into walls, hills into parterres, streams into canals, and paths into geometrical figures. But Beauty is no child of Reason or of the Intellect. Nature demonstrates that 'Proportion is not the cause of Beauty in Vegetables' (*Enquiry*, III/2). Perfection is not the point. Steeped in the tradition of eighteenth-century sceptics such as David Hume, Burke stressed the limitations of our rational constructions, but looked on this very limitation as the essence of Beauty.

The impossibility of grasping the whole becomes the main attraction of Brown's gardens. To spare us anxiety and its obverse, stifling boredom, the English garden provides gradual change. Endless repetition and sudden contrasts prevent relaxation, which is a characteristic effect of Beauty. Hence every straight line in the landscape, however natural, is broken by Brown; the contours of the garden are given an irregular appearance, within which winding paths run past rolling lawns that slope down to a wide meandering river or a lake with curving banks reflecting the shapes and colours of the scattered trees – the only symmetry permitted, because set in motion by wind and water.

THE METAPHYSICS OF THE ZIGZAG

Here the total artifice reveals itself
As the total reality.

Wallace Stevens, 'Someone Puts a Pineapple Together'

The English garden does not grant an overall perspective. Time gets the better of space; where the French garden is revealed suddenly to a stationary observer, the English garden opens up gradually to the roving eye. In this connection it makes sense to speak of the metaphysics of the zigzag. The paths lead to a series of surprisingly new vistas or reveal the same elements in a constantly new perspective. The garden is 'fulfilled' as the spectator walks through it.

The central feature is a movement that proves more relaxing than rest, as Burke noted:

> Most people must have observed the sort of sense they have had, on being swiftly drawn in an easy coach, on a smooth turf, with gradual ascents and declivities. This will give a better idea of the Beautiful, and point out its probable cause better than almost anything else.

A tour through the garden combines relaxation with exertion, much like a cradle or a rocking-chair.

As an example of the dynamics of Beauty, Burke mentions, besides the English garden, the area of a woman's throat and breasts, '. . . the deceitful maze through which the unsteady eye slides giddily, without knowing where to fix, or whither it is carried'. The very impossibility of coming to grips with it has become the principal lure of the English garden. The constant tension between the various forms even lends the garden an erotic aspect. One would like lovingly to stroke or embrace the landscape.

Burke refers to the painter William Hogarth, who in *The Analysis of Beauty* (1753) had developed the idea of the sinuous 'line of beauty', a line he had detected in eggs, parsley, pineapples and Chippendale furniture. This serpentine line (which can also enclose a surface or a volume) is the result of an interplay of forces between symmetry and asymmetry. Inner contradiction is the charm of Beauty; folly leaves something to fantasy – provided it is dispensed in measured doses,

'The line of beauty' by William Hogarth. The vignette on the title- page of *The Analysis of Beauty* (London, 1753) is accompanied by a quotation from Milton's *Paradise Lost* (IX, 516-518), in which Satan, disguised as a twisting serpent, tempts Eve: 'So vary'd he, and of his tortuous train, Curl'd many a wanton wreath, in sight of Eve, to lure her eye.'

since too great a contrast would transform the Beautiful into the Sublime, which would transcend our powers of imagination and lead to stupor.

Unlike the French garden organized round the central axis running straight from the view on the château steps to the vanishing-point on the horizon, the English garden is organized round the 'line of beauty', meandering through the landscape without beginning or end. That line promises us no greater harmony, no resolution of all the contradictions in a transcendent point, but a *concordia discors*, an order in which disorder plays a positive role. The serpentine line in particular lends the garden a paradisiacal aspect.

In short, the metaphysics of the zigzag is based on an artifice, thanks to which an immanent limitation guarantees the success of the garden. From the ground rises a roguish ha-ha; *prata rident*, the meadows laugh.

THE MORAL

Ha ha.
Bosse-de-Nage

The word 'paradise' in Persian originally meant both 'garden' (in the sense of enclosure, a space marked off inside nature), and also 'dwelling of the fortunate'. For centuries mankind has tried in vain to combine these two aspects. The art of gardening is nothing if not an endless series of abortive attempts to transform nature into a pleasure ground. In a sense, every garden prevents itself from becoming a paradise. The garden foils the garden.

But Lancelot Brown knew how to turn this foolish impasse into an avenue of escape by using nature as her own garden. This empty gesture precludes frustration without leading to complete satisfaction. Precisely because it leaves something to be desired, the garden is felt to be natural. The English garden succeeds in its very failure: there lies the 'ha-ha' that secretly accompanies every line of beauty.

Wherever the world appears to be self-evident, we do well to go in search of the ha-ha, the point where order has left room for the folly around which it revolves.

EPILOGUE

In 1979 the Victoria and Albert Museum in London held an exhibition devoted to garden history. In vain did spectators look for the gardens of Capability Brown among the many maps and drawings. A small sign announced that his work was

> . . . an aberration lasting only half a century, depriving the English of the sort of complicated flowery gardens that they love. *Le jardin anglais* refers to the time when the English lost their heads and scrapped their gardens. [. . .] His art and genius consisted solely in modulating ground, water and trees.

Certainly Brown was not concerned with picturesque constituents. He radically eliminated all formal gardens based on the Italian, Dutch

Ha Ha Road

and French models. He was not interested in flowers, urns and other frivolities, but with the great line of beauty.

Brown's paradoxical garden cannot be distinguished from nature. His garden coincides with the empty space in which gardens are normally laid out. The 'empty' garden is not only at odds with other gardens, but with the entire genre. In short, in the species 'English garden', the genus 'garden' clashes with its own opposite.

Hence, it is not pure paradox that Brown's 'invisible' garden was conspicuously absent from this exhibition. The Victoria and Albert Museum felt unable to give space to a garden that subverted the genre. At the same time, however, this blemish on the art of landscape design serves as a benchmark: the genre can only legitimize itself by distancing itself from a garden that negates the garden.

FIVE

SIMPLETONS IN HELL

THE HELL OF FOOLS

According to to Lucretius (*De rerum natura*, III, 978–1023), all punishments meted out in the Underworld should be treated as allegory:

> And, verily, those tortures said to be
> In Acheron, the deep, they are all ours
> Here in this life.
> (trans. W. E. Leonard)

Tantalus, in terror of the great stone suspended over his head as he
thirsts and hungers after water and food, embodies mankind plagued
by an unfounded fear of the gods and the blows of fate. Tityus, whose
liver is eternally torn at by two vultures, represents men tortured by
lust, riven by jealousy and corroded by fear. Sisyphus' vain attempts to
roll a rock up a steep hill exemplify futile attempts to subdue the
people. The Danaïds, who have to fill a bottomless vessel with water,
personify man's vain pursuit of pleasure.

Lucretius places hell not in the hereafter, but in life on earth. Fear
is the punishment for our blind desires:

> 'Tis thence
> That fear of punishments defiles each prize
> Of wicked days.

We are afraid of penance, imprisonment or martyrdom; otherwise
we suffer from remorse, regret and a bad conscience. Punishment is
compounded by the fear that our suffering may be vain and that
things will become worse after death.

Of truth,
The life of fools is Acheron on earth.

However, Lucretius says nothing about the secret enjoyment lurking in our endless, vain attempts to satisfy our desires – about pleasure in displeasure. That bliss is reserved for the poor in spirit. The realization that all our striving is hopeless, that we strive for the sake of striving, turns earthly existence into hell.

ATARAXIA

There is no hell other than fear, which, moreover, is inseparably bound up with our existence. Fear mars our pleasure, but at the same time keeps the world turning. In fear of death, we throw ourselves into life. Mortal fear begets our blind and insatiable desire for sex, power and glory, which in turn elicits fear of punishment, pain and . . . death. This is the vicious circle in which we are trapped. The tension between mortal fear and lust for life is the basis of existential hell. Fear of death ultimately leads to hatred of life.

The only way out of this inferno is ataraxia, emotional tranquillity. The Epicurean tries to rid himself of his delusions by standing aloof from life and by curbing his passions. But even this attempt to become reconciled with existence contains a self-destructive element. In the extreme case, ataraxia is a form of living death, a variant of the ultimate folly: doing nothing for fear of doing something stupid. Afraid of life, the Epicurean longs secretly for death.

Lucretius committed suicide at the age of 45.

BOEOTIAN HELL

There is a marked correspondence between jokes about the stupidity of the people of Gotham or Kampen and the punishments meted out in the Greek Underworld:

> The stupid townspeople scoop up water with a sieve. The Danaïds!

The transporting of the millstone. Woodcut from *Das Schiltbürgerbuch* (1680)

The townsmen drag the logs they have already carried down the mountain back to the top in order to roll them down, which is easier than carrying them. Sisyphus!

In their search for 'the inn on the other side of the road', the townsfolk keep crossing the street. Tantalus!

Lest he lose the millstone, a townsman puts his head through the hole before he rolls the stone down the hill. The scene calls to mind the fate of Ixion, who was bound to a constantly revolving wheel of fire.

The townsmen when out at sea push against the mast to make the ship sail faster. Hercules, who keeps walking about in Tartarus with a permanently drawn bow!

Boeotiana are no awkward caricatures of human existence but reflect the hell hidden in our daily lives: our foolish, automatic actions have order as their side effect, provided only we are unaware of their madness and act in the belief that we are pursuing some distant objective. The Boeotian hell is revealed to all who develop an 'eye for stupidity', for what Flaubert has called 'this terrible talent' that puts an end to all *joie de vivre*.

THE GATE OF HELL

All hope abandon, ye who enter here
Dante, *Inferno*

Zeus presented mankind with a sealed vessel containing everything that is good. Driven by curiosity, man opened the vessel, whereupon all the good evaporated and flew back into the heavens. Hope alone remained (Babrius, *Aesop's Fables*).

In a mysterious variant, Zeus punishes man for the theft of fire, by presenting Epimetheus with Pandora, the 'woman of all gifts'. The gods had endowed Pandora with many charming and beguiling attributes, including a jar filled with evil. Encouraged by Epimetheus ('he who thinks afterwards'), she opened the jar, wherupon all sorts of disasters and afflictions spread through the world, leaving only Hope behind. (Hesiod, *Works and Days*). Or, looked at in a different light: Pandora deprived man of all hope, turning life into hell.

Epimetheus and Pandora opening the jar, by John Flaxman

The Gate of Hell (1880–90) by Auguste Rodin, plaster relief in the Musée d'Orsay, Paris

We also find disenchantment in the biblical myth of the Fall of Man. By eating of the forbidden fruit, Adam and Eve gained the ability to distinguish between good and evil. Their foolish act lent them the insight to realize that they had behaved foolishly. And, with that knowledge, their mortality too became a reality. In short, the acquisition of intelligence was a sin that went hand in hand with a fatal upheaval. Paradise would never return to earth. Our fruitless attempts to restore harmony turn our existence into a Boeotian joke.

On the other hand, our culture is nothing but the result of vain attempts to recover paradise. Or, putting it more strongly, the structural lack is an additional attraction of life on earth – happiness is found in desire, not in fulfilment . . . Yet this works only when unrecognized.

The reverse is symbolized by Dante's Gate of Hell. Above it is written in dark letters: 'All hope abandon, ye who enter here.' This imperative may be considered a riddle: a world without hope turns into hell. The gate stands alone in a forest, like a triumphal arch, which also leads to nothing. The lone gate marks a change in perspective from hope to fear. Fear leads to hell; we die of fear. On the other side of the gate there ought therefore to be the inscription: 'While there is hope, there is life.' Hope opens up prospects, lends a semblance of depth to our banal, Boeotian actions.

This is also reflected in *The Gate of Hell*, the huge bronze door that Auguste Rodin designed as the entrance to the Musée des Arts Décoratifs in Paris. From the summit *The Thinker* (also known as *The Poet* or *Virgil*) contemplates the suffering of damned mankind in the pose of a melancholic. This may be looked on as a satirical protest by Rodin, a declared champion of pure art: on entering the Musée des Arts Décoratifs through the Gate of Hell, all hope abandon. But the accusation is cast in the form of a gate, and as such is an example of applied art. The joke is that Hell does not lie behind the gate, but is depicted on it. Hell is enshrined in the gate; the museum itself was never built.

THE FINAL ANAMORPHOSIS

The mind is its own place, and in it self
Can make a Heav'n of Hell, a Hell of Heav'n.
Milton, *Paradise Lost*

Triumphal arches seem to provide a glimpse of past military glory, but in fact they are absurd monuments attempting to place the traumatic horrors of war in a meaningful context after the event, as witness the Arc de Triomphe in Paris. Veterans of the First World War will tell you that this colossal lump of stone embodies the French spirit. But with the 'eye for stupidity' we see nothing but crude allegories: Napoleon dressed as a Roman, grey tombstones bearing the names of officers, the glorification of battles in such obscure places as Ulm, Austerlitz and Jena, a lifeless unknown soldier, and an eternal flame. The triumphal arch stands like a dead letter in the midst of the heedless traffic endlessly racing around it. The arch serves as a frame for its own hollowness. It is a monument to the folly of all the cunning tricks that hold the nation together.

Seen through the 'eye of the intellect', by contrast, the triumphal arch stands for the human capacity to take courage by recourse to illusion. This trifling difference makes a world of difference. Depending on your point of view, the arch is a monument to the futility of hope, or a triumphal gate for the vanity that keeps hope alive.

This becomes even clearer in the Grande Arche, located not far from the Arc de Triomphe. The Grande Arche is not filled with representations of the glorious past, but has large mirrored walls reflecting the dynamic reality. Here lies the ultimate delusion: on the one hand the Grande Arche is a monument to the vanity of life; on the other hand, it reflects the world as its own triumph.

THE HAUNTED HOUSE

Dante, accompanied by Virgil, is about to enter Hell. Having read the inscription over the gate, 'All hope abandon' (*Lasciate ogni speranza*), Virgil advises Dante to abandon all fear (*lasciate ogni sospetto*). Seen clearly, life without hope is hell, but Hell without fear is a fairground attraction. Dante is on a tour of disaster sites; his visit has something perverse about it. Not that he enjoys all the misery he encounters. He does not share Tertullian's view that watching the suffering of sinners in Hell is a fitting reward for the virtuous. Gloating is not Dante's way. Nor does he agree with St Thomas Aquinas, who rejoices in the existence of Hell because 'just punishment is love', a text that is sometimes quoted to explain another cryptic inscription above the Gate of Hell:

> To rear me was the task of power divine,
> Supremest wisdom, and primeval love.

Dante is deeply affected by the suffering of the damned. He weeps at what he sees, but at the same time he is unable to turn his eyes away. In a sense his enjoyment is more than sheer gloating. He takes pleasure in displeasure. He is fascinated, not because hell is so exotic, but because it reminds him of the folly that is the mystical basis of the society in which he lives. Hell's punishments reflect our cruel struggle for existence. He feels safe in the contrast with the misery that makes the precariousness of his comfortable position tangible.

Hell is not a city of sorrow and pain in an otherwise harmonious society, far from it. Civilization is a castle in the air, a fictitious paradise in the hell of everyday life. But the revelation that Hell does not exist, that there is no difference between Dante and the wretches milling all round him, would put an end to his wry shudders and result in stupor.

This permits another reading of the inscription above the gate: the fiction of Hell is a means of reconciling us to our daily lives, and as such bears witness to the 'supremest wisdom, and primeval love'.

We can see now why *Inferno* is the most popular part of the *Divine Comedy*. Much as Dante is shepherded by Virgil, so the reader of Dante is taken on a tour of Hell. Virgil leads the way 'with pleasant looks'.

THE GIFT OF DISCERNMENT

Beyond the Gate of Hell, Dante meets people who have lost 'il ben dell'intelletto', the divine gift of discernment. In religious terms, this is the power to see God; in philosophical (Aristotelian) terms it is the intuitive grasp of the truth.

In paradise, the intellect is not needed, because every action is innocent, but outside paradise the intellect is indispensable: reason, nous, lends coherence to our picture of the world, puts everything into perspective with an eye to the Highest Good, the *summum bonum*.

In Hell we meet those who have renounced this gift of their own free will, and who are being punished for it with unimaginable tortures. This too allows of a different reading: for those who lose their reason the world becomes hell.

By the side of these colourful sinners, who have squandered their

82

Domenico di Micchelino, *Dante as the Poet of 'The Divine Comedy'* (1465), tempera on panel, Florence Cathedral. Dante, the Gate of Hell and the wretched souls can be seen on the left

God-given powers by choosing evil, there are the wretches who have sinned against their intellect by refusing to choose altogether. This is the foolish rabble Dante first sees when he has passed through the Gate of Hell.

LIMBO

Conducted by Virgil, Dante steps into hell. In the vestibule, even before they reach the Acheron, or Limbo, on a dark plain under a starless sky, an enormous crowd runs perpetually after a whirling flag, pursued by wasps and hornets. The tumult created by these lamenting wretches sounds like a sandstorm.

These are the anonymous shades, the nonentities without blame or fame who do not merit a name. These unfortunates, these failures, these wringers of hands, have sinned by failing to choose, by not even choosing not to choose. They were neither good nor bad. Among them is a group of fallen angels who were neither rebellious nor true to God, but who stood to one side, wholly immersed in their own concerns.

The starless sky stands for the impossibility of finding one's way. The whirling flag symbolizes the vacillations of the undecided. The sandstorm represents their great number, sterility and vanity. The wasps and hornets stand for man's futile hustle and bustle.

These wretches, 'who ne'er lived', are rejected by Heaven and Hell alike. They fall outside the classification of sins and virtues. They are atopic, peculiar. Their eccentricity does not lie in their oddness, but in their monstrous greyness. They deserve neither name nor place. Compared to them, sinners have every right to gloat.

The living dead are doomed to roam eternally between this world and the hereafter. Their blind lives are so mean that they even envy the fate of those tortured in Hell, who at least know their place and punishment, and know what is coming. Their punishment reflects their sin. Not knowing feeds the wretches' fears; this form of torture has been reserved for those who refuse to know right from wrong. For Christians, evil was the source of all the world's misery, but by assigning a place to the 'living dead', Dante also embraced the view of the Greeks, for whom evil springs from folly and ignorance.

Virgil urges Dante to pass them by. Watching the throng of wretched souls is doing them too much honour. 'Fame of them the world hath none.'

THE BLOT

Those who have crossed
With direct eyes, to death's other Kingdom
Remember us – if at all – not as lost
Violent souls, but only
As the hollow men
The stuffed men.

T. S. Eliot, *The Hollow Men*

Not sinners, but the 'living dead' are the blot on Creation. Their 'sin' (which is not specified) is that of acting dumb, foolishness, the passive longing for stupidity. Hollow men allow themselves to be lived. You have only to think of conformists, floating voters, the silent majority, the herd that thoughtlessly follows the latest fancy, opportunists who trim their sails to the wind, people without an opinion, indifferent crowds and cowards who do not commit themselves but run with the hares. They do not deserve a name; no-man's-land is their destination. The real reason, however, why they are doomed to oblivion is that the folly of the Creation is made manifest in them. It is precisely the Boeotian behaviour of the masses that ultimately decides what is generally deemed to be good or evil. Fools demonstrate the hidden truth of the established order: that the separation of the sheep from the goats is arbitrary, that it does not rest on a deliberate choice but on the passive observance of rules and laws.

Since that realization would prove fatal to religion and to the system on which it is based, we turn the tables on it; we behave as if fools disturbed the established order by refusing to choose. Thus the Boeotian aspect of the established order becomes an extra stimulus, an ethical spur to choose, to think and to use our free will. It is only in opposition to fools that we endow our choices with meaning. Compared with the cowards who stand aloof, even sinners begin to look heroic. And so the folly of the Creation turns into a touchstone of principled action, be it moral or immoral.

Lucifer's groin marks the core of Hell, while the whirling foolish rabble in the margins touches on the very core of Creation. The living dead are so fascinating because they remind us of the hollowness, of the Boeotian hell hidden at the heart of the established order. Small wonder that Virgil grows agitated and tells us to pay no heed to them.

THE PARADISE OF FOOLS

They know not nor will understand
In darkness they walk on,
The Earth's foundations all are mov'd
And out of order gone
Psalm 82 (in Milton's translation)

On his journey through Chaos to the Garden of Eden, Satan lands in the outermost sphere of the recently created universe and reflects on his next task: to bring about the Fall of Man. At his feet lies the *primum mobile*, the dark crust containing all the stars and planets. Staring at this 'windy Sea of Land', Satan has a striking vision of the future: he sees an enormous mass of floating men, including monks and priests surrounded by relics, indulgences and rosaries; hermits and pilgrims who sought God on Earth; builders of Babel who raised a tower to heaven; Empedocles who tried to hasten the transmigration of his soul by flinging himself into the flames of Etna, and Cleombrotus, who leapt into the sea to enjoy Plato's Elysium.

All of them are naïve men who try vainly to secure their place in the hereafter while still on Earth. They are rewarded according to the futility of their actions. Like soap bubbles they rise from the Earth past the seven planets, through the sphere of the fixed stars and the crystalline sphere to land on the *primum mobile*.

A glimmer of light from Elysium shores up their hope of eternal salvation; but when they set foot on the stairs of the Heavenly Jerusalem they are 'upwhirl'd aloft', the sport of winds, into a Limbo large and broad, since called the The Paradise of Fools.

Because their deeds spring not so much from wickedness as from infantile vanity and pretension, they are not sentenced to Hell but assigned a place in Limbo, the destination of foolish souls since time immemorial. They call it Paradise because they know no better; the poor in spirit do not realize that their existence 'hangs in the air' and delude themselves that they are on the way to the Kingdom of God.

This story is taken from Milton's *Paradise Lost* (III, 418–96). The topical critique of Papists, the grotesque style, the sketchy character and the strange, isolated position of this satire were so much in conflict with the rest of the strictly and harmoniously constructed epic poem that some critics felt it must have been added by a different author.

From which perspective can we see the importance of this flaw in Milton's work?

THE CEILING OF STUPIDITY

During his visit to Italy in 1638, Milton became familiar with Pietro da Cortona's apotheosis ceiling in the Palazzo Barberini. Cortona had recently put the final touches to a work in which Divine Providence bestows eternal glory and immortality on Pope Urban VIII and his family.

Some years later in London, Milton saw Rubens's ambitious ceiling painting, *The Triumph of King James and the Stuart Monarchy*, undertaken for the new Banqueting Hall, when, as secretary for foreign

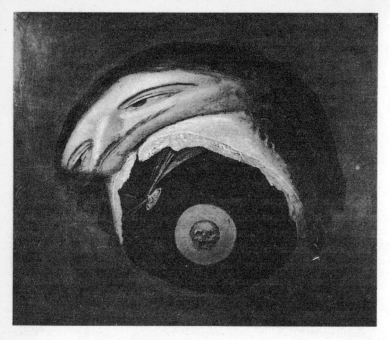

Anamorphosis of Charles I. English School, 1660

languages to the new-formed republican Council of State, he was assigned a room in Whitehall, shortly after the beheading of Charles I in 1649 . . .

In a whirling representation *di sotto in su*, we see the princes of Church and State being raised up to Heaven by angels, surrounded by the symbols of their worldly power and by allegorical figures representing their virtues, such as Piety, Justice and Statecraft. At the edge of the ceiling, heretics are depicted as Giants being expelled from the composition by Minerva, the embodiment of Wisdom.

At least as important is the illusive manner in which the rulers are raised to Heaven. *Quadratura* not only renders their ascension visible, but also makes this metaphysical event tangible. The perspective representation draws the spectator's eye into the freedom of infinite space. Seeing is believing. We forget that we are looking at a ceiling, which is nevertheless a prerequisite of the illusion of infinite space. The aesthetics of *stupore* frees us from our earthly limitations and provides a foretaste of heavenly bliss.

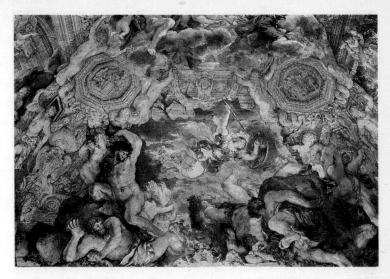

Minerva expelling the giants. Pietro da Cortona, detail from *The Triumph of Divine Providence* (1638–9), fresco, Palazzo Barberini, Rome

Often a point is marked on the floor from which such a scene gains special depth and meaning. As soon as we leave the marked spot, the spectacle takes an unexpected turn: all the verticals become horizontals. Such concepts as upside down and back to front become meaningless. Not only does the apparent order seem to collapse, the dizzying effect raises doubts about the foundations of the world without this perspective. We are in danger of losing our balance; our dumb amazement gives us an impression of the Last Judgment.

The designers, for the most part Jesuit, saw this method as a lesson for those who had adopted the wrong position towards the true faith. In addition, the central point served as a metaphor for royal absolutism and the infallibility of the Pope.

As a republican and a Puritan, Milton rejects this point of view. He steps to one side and so unmasks the foolishness of this illusionary pivot. 'Foolish' because the foolishness goes unnoticed, unless you move from the designated spot, which derives its significance in retrospect from the system based on it. Milton discards this fascinating fallacy. The oblique view robs men inflated with ambition of any prospects. Harmony turns into farce. The exalted figures stumble as if . . .

'Africa', Andrea Pozzo, detail from *The Triumph of St Ignatius of Loyola* (1691–4), fresco, S Ignazio, Rome

> a violent cross-wind from either Coast
> Blows them transverse ten thousand Leagues awry
> Into the devious Air.

Seen in this light, the apotheosis ceiling is an illustration of the Paradise of Fools. The painting immortalizes their fall.

THE WILL TO BE STUPID

The blind Milton used the *stupore* technique to depict stupidity. Seen in the correct perspective, the apparently incongruous passage in Book III of *Paradise Lost* (in which the questions of free will and pre-destination play a central role) turns out to be an anamorphosis of the apotheosis ceiling, that outstanding symbol of self-exaltation, the original sin for which Satan was expelled from Heaven and Adam and Eve from Paradise.

Milton challenged the belief that by his own actions man can win a place in the hereafter. His view was that this was a matter of divine grace. By assigning a place to foolishness in his work, Milton recalls the

Andrea Pozzo, *The Triumph of St Ignatius of Loyola*

limits of human understanding and points to the indefinite space in which our hypothetical constructs, including his own visionary epic, are floating.

The triumph of the intellect is based on a folly whose effects only last while it goes unrecognized. *Esse est non percipi.* If we do not want to lose the ground under our feet, then we must stay dumb when confronting the stupidity at the heart of all systems promising wisdom.

Milton lacked this will to be stupid.

APPENDIX: THE APOTHEOSIS OF A GNAT

'In the rose-red East, Aurora flung open the purple door of her rose-filled rooms. Driven away by the Morning Star, the stars took to flight, as Phaeton's glorious sun chariot rose on the horizon. At long last, the day of my triumph had dawned. Gargantuan Idolatry and Ignorance were cast into the darkness, followed by the serpents of Calumny, as I found myself lifted up into the light by seven angels. On either side, the four Continents appeared in all their splendour. Black Africa, seated on her crocodile, an elephant tusk in her hand; the brightly feathered America on her jaguar; Asia, decked with fruit and pearls, on her camel, and crowned Europe on her horse, all emptied the Horn of Plenty over me. Mighty wings carried me into an infinite heaven. To the sweet sounds of zephyrs with their shawms, harps and cymbals, I rose through gold-rimmed clouds, surrounded by red-cheeked putti bearing my sceptre and golden crown on a carmine cushion. Chronos unveiled the virginal coats of arms of my illustrious forebears. Mars offered me the laurel wreath, Arachne and the seven Liberal Arts paid me homage, Fame proclaimed my glory on her trumpet.

Just as I was about to behold God in all His holy glory, you caught my eye. Oh, winged wrath, vigilant vengeance, how cunningly you found your way through the maze of dark folds in the gossamer curtain surrounding my royal couch, to awaken me from my proud dreams. Half blinded, I guide myself by your unvaried song, to give you thanks for your benefaction. You, who planted my feet on this muddy Earth, I shall raise up to Heaven. Blessed are you, parvulus umoris alumnus, who, sated with my noble blood, have sought repose on the smooth heaven of my bed. Let my silken slipper point the way to your Maker. Farewell.'

Lorenzo Morales, *Morosofia* (Lepe, 1692), trans. from the Spanish by Liesbeth Wiewel and Erica White

SIX

THE GENEALOGY OF DULLARDS

In a Spanish handbook published in 1585, the *Philosofía Secreta de la Gentilidad*, Juan Pérez de Moya (1513–96), noted in his day chiefly as a mathematician, sought to present a Christian, moralistic interpretation of characters and stories from classical mythology. Capítulo XLII of the second volume (squeezed between chapters on Priapus, the god of fertility, and Momus, the god of mockery), catches the eye because it is the only chapter not devoted to the triumphs or disasters of gods and demigods, but concentrates on the fate of dullards, as witness its title: *De la descendencia de los Modorros* ('Modorra' means stupor, dullness). I give here the complete translation of the text, before commenting on it.

ON THE ORIGIN OF DULLARDS

It is said that Lost Time married Ignorance. They had a son named I Thought That.

This son married Youth. They had the following children: I Didn't Know, I Didn't Think, I Didn't Notice, and Who'd Have Thought It.

Who'd Have Thought It married Carelessness. Their children were called That'll Do, It Can Wait Until Tomorrow, There's No Hurry, and The Chance Will Come.

There's No Hurry married the noble lady I Didn't Think. Their children were called I Didn't Give It a Thought, I Know What I'm Saying, I Don't Let Them Fool Me, Don't You Worry, and Leave That To Me.

I Know What I'm Saying married Vanity, and their children were called Like It Or Not, I'll Have My Way, I Demand Respect, You'll Want For Nothing.

You'll Want For Nothing married I Demand Respect. Their children were called Take It Easy and Adversity.

The last-named married Not Many Brains and their children were Nice Work, What's That Got To Do With Him, It Seems To Me, It Isn't Possible, Say No More, You Only Die Once, I'll Get My Way, Time Will Tell, Wait And See, With A Will, No Comment Needed, For The Life Of Me, No Matter What They Say, Whatever The Cost, What Do I Care, We Won't Starve, and It's Not The End Of The World.

I Demand Respect became a widower and married again, this time to Stupidity. When their entire inheritance had been squandered, they said to each other, 'Not to worry, we'll take out a loan and enjoy ourselves for a year. God will provide for the next.' And, advised by You'll Want For Nothing, that is what they did. When the term of the loan expired and they had no money to pay the rent, Illusion took them off to prison. God Will Forgive paid them a visit. Poverty took them to hospital, where the strength of I Demand Respect and I Don't Follow finally gave out. They were buried with Stupidity, their great-grandmother. They left many children and grandchildren, scattered all over the world.

This fable makes clear where the careless, the dullards and the thoughtless come from – those who take no advice, are ruled by their delusions, and live for the day, taking no heed for their future, for what lies in store.

THE POWER OF PALLIATIVES

It was in vogue among Renaissance printmakers to depict such qualities as Beauty, Goodness, Vice or Gluttony as women, generally seated in a landscape filled with objects alluding symbolically to the virtue or vice they personify. Thus Stupidity was sometimes shown as a smiling lady wearing a hat of lead (a reference to *plumbeum ingenium*, a leaden mind) and carrying a small mill, the symbol of grinding thoughts and pointless actions.

Allegorical literature also deals with the adventures of various abstract concepts and their interrelationships. A classic example is the *Psychomachia* by Prudentius (fifth century AD), in which virtues and vices wage war on one another. In Baltasar Gracián's *El Criticón* (1651), Stupidity appears as the sister of Illusion, both of them children of Lies and grandchildren of Ignorance.

The writings of Juan Pérez de Moya, too, list some of the more classic sins, such as Vanity, Ignorance and Stupidity. Side by side with these deadly sins, we are introduced to a less familiar group, consisting of nouns owing their negative connotation to association with certain adjectives, for instance Lost Time and Not Many Brains. But the most striking feature of the cited passage is that it introduces such palliatives as empty phrases and lame excuses, in short, bluff and circumlocution. In his genealogy of stupidity, the author has attempted to analyse the complex structure of this special category of expression.

THE WORD MADE FLESH

We can distinguish three levels in the genealogy. The first is the textual rearrangement. The palliatives are extracted from their original context and fitted into another. One expression is highlighted in another. This device might have led to such elegant constructions as 'I Know What I'm Saying said "I know what I'm saying."' However, the author makes no use of these. The fact that texts appear as central elements of other texts opens up enough giddying perspectives as it is.

Moreover, in the allegorical family tree, the logical nexus between separate statements is reconstructed. The links between cause and effect are more complicated than appears at first sight.

When all is said and done, palliatives appear in the moral context as symbols of an odious attitude of mind. Pat expressions personify various aspects of foolish negligence.

Remarkably enough, we do no great violence to palliatives if we take them out of their natural context. They are mostly offhand, private remarks. In the new context they are admittedly transformed into figures of speech, but allegory leaves their characteristic features intact. Even isolated palliatives reflect an unacceptable mentality. Empty phrases always live a life of their own. Their presence generally signifies the beginning and at the same time the end of a conversation. They are apodeictic, eschew dialogue, leave no room for doubt or contradiction, are deaf to the opinion of others and self-deluding.

Their smug character is emphasized by what are often incestuous interconnections. This inbreeding leads to further degeneration. But though palliatives may frustrate mental development, they allow stupidity to flourish. Procreation leads to growing idiocy and the result is a worldwide diaspora of dullards.

THE TRIUMPH OF POOR EXCUSES

What mentality is being analysed here with the help of palliatives? Less the clash of overt, heroic and provocative sins against order and morality, than covert, everyday, hidden vices. Palliatives veil and embody a furtive attitude. Not the incidental mortal sin, but structural neglect is their central feature, the clear conscience that pulls the wool over its own eyes and is unaware of evil.

Of course, these venial sins, too, can be traced back to widespread mortal sins such as Sloth, Prodigality and Vanity, but their treacherous power lies precisely in their infinite variety. It is the sum of these inconspicuous personal sins that ultimately undermines morality at large.

The great power of the passage quoted lies in its presentation of this fatal course of development. We are not given a sensational account of dramatic acts of heroism, but a matter-of-fact summary of everyday events such as marriage and reproduction. The cumulative nature of the piece raises a laugh. The constant repetition of events, given extra emphasis by the bureaucratic account of the register of marriages, has an almost biblical gloss

Not Sloth (*Desidia*) or Vanity (*Superbia*), but the reproductive urge (a conservative form of *Luxuria*) is crucial to the final triumph of excuses. Palliatives succeed in what heroes and gods can only achieve with the greatest difficulty. Through sleep and coitus they conquer the world. Under the cloak of palliatives, stupidities gain control of our existence. Our everyday actions in particular seem to have a fatal effect. Their mystical power does not lie in their individual quality but in their number. Human stupidity and monogamy go far beyond divine cunning and debauchery.

The corrupting palliatives have thus finally been assigned their rightful place in mythology. At long last, the decisive role of this neglected group has received due recognition.

Towards the end, the author dwells at some length on the fate of I Demand Respect. After his first wife (and sister), You'll Want For Nothing, died an untimely death, he marries Stupidity. Intemperance (*Gula*) proves to be their downfall. Did the author perhaps miscalculate? I Demand Respect seems suddenly married to I Didn't Notice, a distant forebear, while his second wife, Stupidity, is suddenly said to be his grandmother. And how is it possible that You'll Want For Nothing is resurrected from the grave to advise the young couple on the best use of their capital?

More important, however, is the sudden appearance of a key figure of the Baroque from the wings: Illusion takes the stage to seal the characters' fate. Illusion (*engaño*, delusion, self-deceit, deception) has Disillusion (*desengaño*, reflection, enlightenment, healthy disenchantment) as its classical counterpart. This couple generally presides over morality. In the theatre of palliatives, by contrast, Illusion reigns supreme. Lost Time and Ignorance blithely enter into marriage. Their union does not lead to understanding or insight, but to mental indolence, arrogance, vague conjectures and the birth of palliative devices.

The last act is no more than an obligatory turn, in which morality may only take the stage to proclaim that shortsightedness and inattention lead to certain perdition. However, this announcement cannot disguise the fact that morality and reason are impotent. The death of I Demand Respect puts an end to the genealogy, not because Stupidity is buried with him but because the infinite ramification of her pedigree can no longer be surveyed. Morality has lost its hold on existence, and is in danger of being overrun by Stupidity's descendants.

THE HOUR OF ALL

Following the example of Juan Pérez de Moya, Francisco de Quevedo wrote a *Genealogy of Dullards*. Later, in 1635, he described the purveyors of empty phrases in *La Hora de Todos y la Fortuna con Seso* (The Hour of All and Fortuna with Brains), a grand allegory in which the pagan theme of Fortuna is used to illustrate a world in crisis.

Jupiter summons all the gods to call Fortuna to account. Blind Fortuna appears with a stick and a guide dog. She moves forward on a ball and, like the hub of a wheel, is surrounded by a tangle of wires, strings and ribbons that become entwined and disentwined as she turns. She is followed by Opportunity, a woman with a barbarous expression and a bald skull ('a mirror for swallows'). A single thick lock of hair hangs over her forehead; we must seize Opportunity whenever she appears, for once she has passed, her lock can no longer be grasped.

Opportunity and Contrition, grisaille fresco from the School of Andrea Mantegna (*c.* 1500), Palazzo Ducale, Mantua. In this variant Opportunity (*Occasio*) teeters with a winged foot on a ball. She is blinded by her lock of hair. Contrition (*Poenitentia*) remains behind her. True learning (*Vera Eruditio*), standing on a solid foundation, protects man from the temptations of Fortuna.

Jupiter argues that the follies of Fortuna have caused mankind to lose faith in the gods and to believe that heaven is empty. She is blamed not so much for her blindness as for her iniquity. For she rewards evildoers and plunges the righteous into misery.

Fortuna pleads that none of this is her fault; she simply scatters her gifts blindly and at random. Opportunity adds that it is up to man to seize her. If anyone comes off second best, it will be due to his own negligence. But man hides his mental indolence and corruption behind platitudes:

Stupidity has spread the following infernal phrases among men:

> Who'd have thought it – I would never have thought so – I didn't notice – I didn't realize – It will have to do – It makes no difference – It leaves me cold – Tomorrow is another day – No

rush – All in good time – I didn't notice – I know what I want – I'm not that stupid – Stop going on like that – It won't kill me – Laughter is the best policy – Don't believe everything you hear – Whatever the cost – It isn't possible – To each his own – God will provide – Patience is its own reward – I'm not the only one – Enough is enough – What business is it of yours? – In my view – That's impossible – Not another word – I can do no more – Time will tell – The world keeps turning – You only die once – What are you thinking of? – Come what may – I speak my mind – We are all in the same boat – I know whom I'm dealing with – That's my business – Wait and see – That's what they say.' And lots of 'buts' and 'maybes'. But the favourite refrain of these blockheads is: 'Come what may!'

These foolish phrases render men arrogant, lazy and slovenly. They are the ice over which I glide, they make my mistress's wheel revolve, and spin the sphere that serves her for a shoe. But when these idiots let me escape, can I be blamed for slipping away?'

Jupiter decides to perform an experiment. He decrees that at four o'clock in the afternoon of 20 June all men will be paid according to their just deserts for an hour. Fortuna lets go of her wheel, which spins across the world, hurling everything into bewildering confusion.

ZERO HOUR

When the bell tolls, the physician turns executioner. The accused changes roles with his guard. Garbage pours into an apothecary's shop, while the jars of pills roll out through the door and into the dustbins. Dustmen armed with brooms and shovels do their bit by throwing painted women with syphilitic noses and dyed hair after them.

A thief who has sunk his fortune into the construction of a luxurious apartment building that he plans to let out, watches brick after brick disappear and the roof tiles fly off. Doors, windows and fences go in search of their rightful owners. The coats of arms on the facade streak off like greased lightning to resume their place in the castles to which the scoundrel has deceitfully attributed his origins.

All that is left is the sign 'Apartments to Let', which now reads: 'Thief to let, homeless, no need to knock, the building no longer stands in the way.'

The empty phrases also return. In Chapter VII, the judges hide their incompetence behind such clichés as 'Come what may' or 'God alone knows'. After the bell has tolled, the judges sentence themselves. Their robes turn into snakeskins, and they hurl themselves at one another.

In Chapter XVI it is the turn of the crooks, who do their best to palm off on each other dud bills of exchange, fake diamonds and stolen silver. To facilitate these swindles they resort to such fine phrases as 'I always call a spade a spade', 'A man's word is his bond', 'My parents taught me right from wrong'. To which the other replies: 'A yea is a yea and a nay is a nay', 'That's the way I happen to be', 'What counts is what you're like deep down'. And then the bell tolls for them as well. Suddenly all these swindlers start believing one another. The one exchanges his fool's gold for forged bills, the other his paste jewels for stolen silver. When they try to sell their newly acquired goods, they are all arrested for fraud.

THE JOVIAL GESTURE

At the hour in which everyone gets his due, the world is turned upside-down. That does not, however, mean that justice is victorious – quite the reverse. All who were poor and humble become possessed by the Devil the moment they come into money. Those who were rich and distinguished suddenly become poor and charitable. Good pluto-crats and bad paupers do not seem to exist in this world.

At the end of his experiment Jupiter concludes that man is so weak he can only cease his evil actions when he absolutely must, not from contrition but from impotence. The reproach that Fortuna favours rogues and punishes the virtuous is not just. Fortune does not smile on the wicked; man becomes wicked when Fortune smiles on him. Depending on the circumstances, man is victim and executioner at one and the same time, deceiver and deceived. Only those are good who have no opportunity to do evil.

Yet, Jupiter does not despair. The instability of the world, of which Fortune is the symbol, is also the expression of Divine Providence. It is up to man to use his free will and insight to profit from the trials to which Heaven subjects him. Fortune is neither inescapable fate nor a blind accident before which man stands powerless. God helps those who help themselves. Wise is the man who bears the blows of fortune patiently and who can take a detached view of happy events. The fools who try to shelve their responsibilities with the help of empty phrases, by contrast, turn into Fortune's playthings.

When Jupiter also adds that he is handing everyone his just deserts, he is not thinking of punishment for the wicked. On the contrary. At the end of the hour, he refrains from sanctions and restores the status quo. The world is delivered back to the whims of Fortune.

> Let Fortuna lead her wheel and ball back onto well-trodden paths. Let her promise rewards to the wise and punishment to the foolish; our infallible providence and sovereign power shall ensure that everyone receives what is allotted to him by Fortune. Her favour or disfavour is not bad in itself, for if only mankind knows how to bear all reverses and how to scorn all favours, both will benefit us. Let him who takes what he receives from her and puts it to bad use blame himself and not Fortune, for she gives freely and without evil intent.

Then the bell tolls the fifth hour, and everything is again as it was.

THE UNITY OF OPPOSITES

For a moment the mind
On distant images dwelled
And entered, like the camel
Through the needle's eye.
In which land did he end up?
On earth – in his own land.
Martinus Nijhoff, *Het uur U* (Zero Hour)

The paradox is characteristic of the Baroque: riches bring comfort but also anxiety; poverty is the source of suffering, but also of peace and serenity. Quevedo, however, goes one step further. Instead of simple opposites such as rich or poor, good or bad, dead or alive, he proclaims the immanent contradiction of existence itself. In *Everyone's Hour* the ambivalent character of the apparently self-evident world is unmasked. Every object contains its own opposite that is undermining and inspiring it at the same time; our enemies are our true friends, sickness is a healthy ordeal, death gives us access to the true life. In this defence of the identity of opposites, the Stoic heritage is given a Christian gloss. It is only in unhappiness that man finds the proper conditions for his happiness.

This dialectical view of existence is reflected in the structure of the work. Every scene consists of two antithetical sections, appearing respectively before and after the hour strikes. This view is also reflected in the paradoxical style. Quevedo plays off the catchphrases – the clichés, which relieve man from thought – against each other, reconciles the irreconcilable and juggles with words. In this way he makes the reader aware of the mendacious nature of the empty slogans masking the paradoxical character of the world. And indirectly, by means of his theoretical fireworks, Quevedo alludes to the fact that man is free to give meaning to his ambivalent existence.

SEVEN

On the Inherent Stupidity of Constitutional Monarchies

A Mirror for Princes
For W. A. van B.

PROLOGUE: THE FROGS WHO WANTED A KING

The frogs, enjoying the freedom of their marshland, petitioned Jupiter to let them have a king who would put an end to the lax morals that prevailed there. With a smile, the father of the gods flung a log into the morass. When they had recovered from the shock, the frogs approached their king, and on examining him took to mocking him. The frogs then asked Jupiter for a proper king, whereupon he threw a water snake into the marsh, which swallowed them all up.

Here we have the two extremes of our society: democracy can degenerate into anarchy while monarchy can end in dictatorship. Aesop's fable illustrates that democracy exists by the grace of a king, provided only that he is no smarter than a log.

The frogs who wanted a king. Naples, 15th-century print

THE FIRST STUPID ACT (A FABLE)

In the beginning was stupidity. Nature confounded herself by giving birth to an idiocy on which our culture is founded: a self-destructive folly manifested itself in mankind. The evenly balanced cycle of blossom and decay hitherto ruled by the instincts, was broken by man's foolhardy longing for a freedom that was no longer natural because reckless, and not yet culture because untamed. In his *Vorlesung über 'Pädagogik'* (1776), Immanuel Kant referred to this primal stupidity, which lurks in the inhospitable realm between nature and culture, as '*Wildheit*', savageness.

> Man has [. . .] by nature so strong a longing for freedom that, once used to it for even a short time, he will sacrifice everything for it.

This folly, for which man risks his own life and that of his species, sets him apart from the beasts:

> Animals use their strength [...] properly, that is, so as not to harm themselves.

Man, by contrast, is the only living being who, at birth, is so stupid as to attract the attention of predators with his cries. Because he lacks natural instincts, man is forced to subject his impetuous savagery to laws with the help of discipline.

Erhard Schön, *Polishing the Rough Men* (1533)

SAVAGENESS AND RUDENESS

Man, according to Kant, is not only savage by nature, but also rude, uncultured, and unable to match means with ends. Roughness or rudeness (*Roheit*), more so even than savageness (*Wildheit*), is close to what Kant understands by stupidity (*Dummheit*): 'Lack of judgment is what is really meant by stupidity.' But in contrast to the dullard, the newlyborn human can be 'unroughened' – whence the term *e-ruditio*.

Unlike discipline, which plays a negative role, teaching constitutes the positive component of education. The two are nevertheless closely related, since it is his perennial savageness that compels man to polish himself.

> Because of his hankering after freedom, man needs to polish his rudeness; animals by contrast do not, thanks to their instincts. [...] An animal is all it is by virtue of its instincts; an external reason has seen to that. Man, however, needs an inner reason. He has no instinct.

Savage stupidity, in short, is an obstacle to culture, which, by definition, has no place for folly. On the other hand, it is the basis of civilization, which is simply the product of a series of more or less successful attempts to come to terms with man's idiocy.

THE SCORPION AND THE TORTOISE

Rudeness can be cured, savageness cannot. This is illustrated by the fable of the tortoise who befriended a scorpion, included in an Indian guide for princes, the *Panchatantra*. When the tortoise gave his friend a lift on his back to help him cross a river, the scorpion tried to kill him with its deadly sting. Shocked, the tortoise asked for an explanation of this foolish act, which might have cost both of them their lives. To which the scorpion replied: 'I could not help myself.'

Remember, this is a fable. Animals are not stupid; men alone act against their better judgement. And that is the crux of the matter: stupidity is not found in the lack of thought, but in doing it anyway.

Folly is an act of absolute freedom, based on nothing but itself. The scorpion does not act for some good reason, but in response to something stronger than itself. What culture has to subdue is not nature but the self-destructive stupidity recurring everywhere and at all times. Man must learn to recognize stupidity in its bewildering dimensions and to develop a *modus vivendi*, a way of coming to terms with it.

THE REVERSAL

Self-destruction is a breach of the unwritten law of nature, which aims at self-preservation. Stupidity poses a fatal threat to man. And since life-threatening stupidity cannot be eradicated without eradicating man himself, a ruse is needed.

Self-destruction is turned into its opposite when disinterested self-sacrifice is declared the highest end of civilization. In this way idiocy is made the kingpin of culture. In essence, this norm is unnatural, because self-destructive: from nature's point of view self-sacrifice is the pinnacle of stupidity. But viewed formally, the norm is no breach of natural law, because man opts paradoxically for self-sacrifice as a means of self-preservation.

Self-sacrifice is a travesty in which stupidity assumes the character of the highest wisdom. Martyrdom is sacred stupidity. Excess becomes the norm. Hence civilization is its own caricature: a form of stupidity become culture, a folly become second nature. This explains why we laugh at jokes in which men endanger their own lives; not because they go against nature, but because their stupidity is so closely bound

Fable and Truth, 'A moral must, to do us good, / Be masked in fable and charm like verse; / Truth pleases less completely nude, / No other virgin in the universe / When slightly clad is better viewed.' Frontispiece engraving for C.-J. Dorat and N.-A. Delalain's *Fables ou allégories osophiques* (1772)

up with the core of the norm: voluntary self-destruction. In the jokes we can see that self-destructive fools lurk behind disinterested, self-sacrificing subjects. Voluntary slavery masks the war of all against all.

2 MAN IS A GRAPE

ECSTACY

> A dog was swimming across a river with a sausage in its
> mouth, when he suddenly saw the reflection in the water of
> another dog with a sausage. Not to be outdone, he dropped his
> own sausage and tried to snatch the other one. But together
> with his own, the other dog's sausage vanished in the water.

Stupidity is not so much the result of faulty perception or fallacious
logic as a form of ecstasy: whenever we try to prove our worth, we are
beside ourselves. This testifies to a blind will to folly, a process in which
we lose sight of ourselves.

SELF-LOVE AND SELF-LIKING

> There once lived a frog in a marsh who thought he was a
> prince, but no one took his croaking seriously. To prove him-
> self, he entered the eleven-town long-distance skating race,
> tried his hand at water-skiing and took up windsurfing. All the
> other frogs laughed at him. Gloomily the frog-prince went on
> splashing about in his puddle until the reeds whispered the
> magic words: water management.

Bernard Mandeville (Rotterdam 1670–1733 London) concluded that
the stupidity underlying our culture was selfishness. All man's thoughts
and actions are naïve or conscious attempts to satisfy passions rooted
in egoism. Hunger, thirst and the sexual urge are born of self-love, an
instinct primarily aimed at self-preservation. Yet how can we explain
suicide? How can egoism possibly drive a man to self-destruction?

Mandeville makes a distinction between Self-love and 'a nameless passion' which he calls Self-liking. Self-love obeys the dictates of nature, and reflects a sense of reality. Self-liking, by contrast, is the ability to cling to illusions. It involves an overestimation of ourselves that arouses a lust for life, even when life does not deserve it. Self-liking protects us from despair. Self-love cannot exist without Self-liking. We are only able to bear reality with the help of fantasies. Deprived of Self-liking, Self-love turns into self-hatred. Hence man can choose suicide out of Self-love, once Self-liking has abandoned him.

However, Self-liking also has a self-destructive aspect. It can make us deaf to the dictates of nature. With 'a full stomach', that is, once our primary needs are satisfied, Self-liking can inspire us to act ruthlessly against our own best interests, for instance to satisfy such a passion as Pride.

Man's tendency to exaggerate his own importance goes hand in hand with a secret doubt. Like seeks like for self-confirmation, yet an excessive display of self-liking leads to mutual aversion. Here we impinge on the stupid crux of civilization: pride stands in the way of pride. Self-liking, and the inner conflict to which it gives rise, kills the fruits of self-liking, and, moreover, constitutes an obstacle to social life. The threat proud people pose to one another forces us to resort to a trick.

THE TRICK

No one can claim to be free of pride without blowing his own trumpet. Pride is ineradicable. That is why we do well to turn pride – for the sake of which man is willing to act against his natural instincts – against itself. Culture teaches us to take pride in concealing our pride. Good Manners were born as a result. Propriety is a form of self-sacrifice, compensated by flattery. 'The Moral Virtues are the Political Offspring which Flattery begot upon Pride.' Flattery leads to virtue. And the greater the show of propriety and the greater the pride, the greater the fear of being put to shame, the greater the display of propriety, and so on. The stroke of genius is that the more pride is concealed, the more pride is satisfied. *Superbia* – according to theologians the prime moral sin – becomes the crux of morality. Pride, excessive self-esteem, supplies the fuel on which the social machinery runs. We gain self-assurance from self-denial.

DUMBING DOWN

Culture is organized round pride and shame with flattery as its instrument, that is, with lies. We encourage this mummery. With pretence, we allow pride free rein. If pride is repressed, it degenerates into cruelty and envy. Propriety replaces the natural, objectionable symptoms of pride with such artifices as personal hygiene, fine clothing, furniture, buildings, paintings, courtesy titles, in short with everything that elicits respect without giving offence. We act as if these manifestations of culture had sprung from noble motives, and propriety teaches us never to challenge that pretence. Over the years, man comes to believe in the virtue of his motives, 'insensible to the hidden Spring that gives Life and Motion to all his Actions'. If only we pretend long enough to act decently, even for indecent motives, we become decent as a matter of course.

HYPOCRISY

Norms are based neither on nature nor on reason, but on passion. Virtues are tricks to satisfy our selfishness. Under the guise of propriety, we sail round the rocks barring the satisfaction of our self-liking. Hypocrisy dogs pride like a shadow. Quite often our cant is not deliberate. Selfishness lurks behind even sincere altruism. Every man deceives himself. Reason, too, is unwittingly guided by passion; all thought is a rationalization of desire. In the end, we even learn to look on egoism as something sinful. For that very reason, the revelation that self-conceit lies at the heart of society is felt as an affront to our self-conceit.

Stupidity reigns where all seems self-evident. We are blind to the role of pride and to its camouflage. Intelligence cannot tear the veil away: pride blinds even the most sensible man to pride.

THE GOOD IN EVIL

The wolf is a wolf to the lamb, and a wolf is a wolf to a wolf. According to Plautus, however, man is a wolf to man, and not a fellow human being ... And Thomas Hobbes wrote: 'Man is to man a kind of God,

J. F. Leopold (1668–1726), *General Masquerade*

man to man is an errant wolf' (*De Cive*, 1642). It is because man is so filled with self-conceit that he poses a threat to himself and to his species.

In short, man is not a political animal, as Aristotle contended. In vain do we look for an innate sense of solidarity in man. But Mandeville does not go as far as Hobbes, who asserts that man is incurably asocial. It is precisely by virtue of his egoism that man has become a social being:

> the Bad and Hateful Qualities of Man, his Imperfections and the want of Excellencies which other Creatures are endued with, are the first causes that made Man sociable.

In short, social evil comes before social virtue. We have to realize

> that what renders him a Sociable Animal, consists not in his desire of Company, Good-nature, Pity, Affability, and other pleasing Graces of a fair Outside; but that his vilest and most hateful Qualities are the most necessary Accomplishments to fit him for the largest, and, according to the World, the happiest and most flourishing Societies.

Culture revolves about vice. Mandeville's motto is 'Private vices, public benefits'. Of course, not every vice is a public virtue. The reverse is true: all 'good' is based on 'evil'. Only when vice becomes a crime against the common good does it have to be punished.

Mandeville dissected his age, the better

> to expose the Unreasonableness and Folly of those, that, desirous of being an opulent and flourishing People [...] are yet always murmuring at and exclaiming against those Vices and Inconveniences, that from the Beginning of the World to this present Day, have been inseparable from all Kingdoms and States that ever were fam'd for Strength, Riches and Politeness, at the same time.

THE FABLE OF THE BEES

In *The Fable of the Bees* (1714) Mandeville takes it nobly upon himself

> to shew the Vileness of the Ingredients that all together com-
> pose the wholesome Mixture of a well order'd Society; in order
> to extol the wonderful Power of Political Wisdom, by the help
> of which so beautiful a Machine is rais'd from the most con-
> temptible Branches.

More precisely, too strong an emphasis on man's goodness has a paralysing effect on society as a whole. The consequence of the banishment of evils is the subject of Mandeville's fable.

Once upon a time there was a flourishing beehive. The bees 'were not Slaves to Tyranny, Nor ruled by wild Democracy', but led by 'Kings, that could not wrong, because, Their power was circumscrib'd by laws'. Within the hive every office and profession was tainted with corruption, 'No Calling was without Deceit'. But the vices of each were subordinated to the well-being of all by an able administration.

> Thus every Part was full of Vice,
> Yet the whole Mass a Paradice.

More pointedly still:

> The Worst of all the Multitude
> Did something for the common Good.

Yet everyone complained about fraud and corruption, especially the rich, who were swindlers themselves. Mercury laughed at their antics, but Jove grew incensed and decided to rid the hive of all fraud.

> The Mask Hypocrisie's flung down,
> From the great Statesman to the Clown;
> And some, in borrow'd Looks well known,
> Appear'd like Strangers in their own.

Suddenly virtue reigned supreme. Judges, lawyers, locksmiths, turnkeys, tipstaffs – all were thrown out of work. Earnings dwindled.

Everyone lived frugally. Luxury disappeared, unemployment rose. The building trade collapsed, the economy went downhill. 'The slight and fickle Age is past; and Cloaths, as well as Fashions last.' Thousands died of starvation. The moral:

> then leave complaints: Fools only strive
> To make a Great and honest Hive.
> T' enjoy the World's Conveniencies,
> Be famed in War, yet live in Ease
> Without great Vices, is a vain
> Eutopia seated in the Brain.

Mandeville wrote his fable not because he expected a change for the better, but because he hoped that

> those who are so fond of the Ease and Comforts, and reap all the Benefits that are the Consequence of a great and flourishing Nation, would learn more patiently to submit to those Inconveniencies, which no Government upon Earth can remedy, when they should see the Impossibility of enjoying any great share of the first, without partaking likewise of the latter.

THE FABLE OF THE SOCIAL CONTRACT

How did man in his natural state, in which he is subject to nothing but the law of self-preservation, arrive at culture, in which he must obey the commands of a communal authority?

Society itself tries to explain its origins by means of a social contract, a pact based on liberty, equality and fraternity: every person submits voluntarily to the rule of society, and society treats every person as part of the whole. As citizens, its members state jointly what they want, the better to attain it as individual subjects. As a result freedom and self-preservation are vouchsafed to all: no one obeys anybody other than himself, and the community protects each one from the selfishness of others.

There is just one tiresome problem: the social contract presupposes the existence of the society it sets out to explain: that is, the presence of individuals who follow the rules of a rational order. In short, the explanation is based on a circular argument, a *petitio principii*. What we have here is a myth intended to disguise the fact that civilization is born out of egoism: 'No Man would keep a Contract longer than that Interest lasted, which made him submit to it.'

Man is by nature neither good nor bad, only stupid. The stability of society is not based on moral sentiment, but on the shrewd use of stupid self-conceit. To that end, the vices and their subtle stratagems, the virtues, were first introduced. Virtues are temporary and indigenous attempts to come to terms with our irrational and timeless egoism. Society, in brief, is not based on communal sentiment but on an asocial folly elevated to the status of an admirable norm with the aid of a trick. Culture is acculturated selfishness. Society is a by-product of fundamentally asocial actions.

Had man been endowed with an instinctive love of his neighbours, there would be no wars. And had he preserved his primitive simplicity he would never have become a social being.

THE PUNCH-BOWL

Nature designed 'Man for Society, as she has made Grapes for Wine'. Fermentation is the effect of togetherness, not its cause. Society is not the product of an innate communal sense; sociability is the product of an astutely managed society. *Fabricando fabri fimus*, practice makes perfect. Society becomes social when everyone obeys the law, regardless of his or her asocial motives.

But all this happens unconsciously. The knowledge that society rests on calculating egoism is not conducive to morality. For that reason we fool one another that we are keeping the social contract out of a communal feeling. Ignorance and stupidity are essential elements of social equilibrium, as appears from Mandeville's comparison of the 'Body Politick' to a 'Bowl of Punch':

> Avarice should be the sow'ring, and Prodigality the sweetning of it. The Water I would call the Ignorance, Folly and Credulity of the floating insipid Multitude; whilst Wisdom, Honour, Fortitude, and the rest of the sublime Qualities of Men, which separated by Art from the dregs of Nature, the fire of Glory has exalted and refin'd into a Spiritual Essence, should be an

Mistress World: Amiability itself from the front, scorn lies in wait behind. A print of 1700

equivalent to Brandy. [. . .] Experience teaches us, that the
Ingredients I named judiciously mixt, will make an excellent
Liquor, lik'd of and admir'd by Men of exquisite Palates.

3 THE TRIFLING DIFFERENCE

THE TRUTH OF THE TRUTH

In *La Philosophie découvrant la Vérité*, an allegory from the Enlightenment, we see Philosophy (bearing the torch of reason) unveiling the Social Contract as the basis of all culture. However, if we look more closely at the illustration, we see that for her part, naked Truth is trying to hide something. Beneath her right foot she is silencing a mask, blindfolded and with the ears of an ass – Stupidity, which is the real basis of our civilization.

A bust of Jean-Jacques Rousseau can be seen in the background.

Philosophy discovering
the Truth
An 18th-century print

MAN IS GOOD BUT NOT STUPID

According to Rousseau, the first man to fence in a piece of land and to hit upon the idea that 'this is mine' and who, moreover, found people foolish enough to believe him, was the founder of society. This cunning distinction between thine and mine posed a threat to natural freedom.

The social contract was a counter-ploy to prevent murder and mayhem, a method of coming to terms with this type of idiocy (particularism in the strictest sense of the word). The social contract involves the abandonment of self-interest for the sake of the common weal. However, that does not put a stop to the idiocy – quite the contrary.

According to Rousseau, man is good by nature, but no fool. Near is my coat but nearer is my shirt. Or rather: 'Why is it that . . . all continually will the happiness of each one, unless it is not a man who does not think of "each" as meaning him?' (*Du contrat social*). Every individual thinks secretly of himself when he speaks on behalf of all. This shortsighted egoism poses a permanent threat to the state while yet being its mystical foundation. Equality before the law originates in the 'preference each man gives to himself, and accordingly in the very nature of man'.

THE LEGISLATOR

We do not obey the law because it is advantageous to do so; rather, the law becomes an advantage if everyone obeys it. But how can uncivilized man be persuaded in the first place to obey a completely unprofitable law? If the masses had been endowed by nature with the ability to appreciate the benefits of the law, no social contract would have been needed: 'Men would have to be before law what they should become by means of the law.' In short, social sentiment would have preceded the institution of the state. But the 'blind multitude' is at first too foolish to appreciate the principles of political science. It fails to grasp the advantages of self-sacrifice.

Rousseau called a mythical legislator into being. To persuade men of the advantages of the social contract, this first lawgiver cannot and may not resort to violence or argument. If he did so, he would be flying in the face of democratic principles, even before the emergence of a society in the true sense of the word. Only a law adopted by the people themselves can be binding upon them. To avoid the suspicion of covert self-interest, the legislator must wield no political power, only the power of the word. As a demagogue, he presents objects as 'they ought to appear to the masses'. He teaches the people to 'discover what they want'. He holds up a mirror to men in which they can view themselves as a part of the whole. His trick is a reversal of the actual state of affairs: he pretends that the social contract is a purely formal confirmation of an existing situation. He acts as if the consequence of the contract, society, were the cause of the contract. The identity of society, which he presents as an incontestable fact, only exists by the grace of his fiction. He turns a random collection of men into a unit by virtue of the fairy-tale proclaiming this unity. With the help of fables and the appeal to higher powers he misleads them into believing his fiction until it becomes a reality.

THE FOURTH KIND OF LAW

What we opprobriously call stupidity, though not an enlivening quality in common society, is nature's favourite resource for preserving steadiness of conduct and consistency of opinion.
Walter Bagehot, *The Inquirer* (1852)

Arguments may perhaps convince the wolf in man of the advantages of the law, but he does not really seem to care, whereas the sheep in man is full of good will but has no idea of the mechanics of state. This is no real problem because the legislator tacitly applies a type of law more powerful than constitutional law, civil law and criminal law combined, 'a fourth [law], most important of all, which is graven not on tablets of marble or brass, but on the hearts of the citizens'. He invokes laws that preserve the spirit of the constitution, and that, unnoticed, replace the power of the state with the force of habit – morals and customs as well as current opinions (*doxai*). These are the foolish but practical keystones of society. The success of all other laws hinges on them. Even if the social contract were to be dissolved, they would guarantee the survival of the general will.

THE ROD AND THE SERPENT

To carry the common people along, those who refused to be swayed by his wise opinions, the legislator decided to put his verdicts into the mouths of the gods. While it is not given to all men to let the gods speak, every one of us can write on stone tablets or buy an oracle:

> He whose knowledge goes no further may perhaps gather round him a band of fools; but he will never found an empire, and his extravagances will quickly perish with him. Idle tricks form a passing tie; only wisdom can make it lasting.

In fact, the opposite is the case: the permanence of the effect transforms the founding gesture retrospectively from an unimaginably foolish trick into a wisdom beyond all understanding . . .

Thus, according to Rousseau, the 'Judaic Law, which still subsists, and that of the child of Ishmael . . . still proclaim the great men who laid them down; and, while the pride of philosophy or the blind spirit of faction sees in them no more than lucky impostures, the true political theorist admires, in the institutions they set up, the great and powerful genius which presides over things made to endure.' In other words, the share of inspired deception in our civilization is greatly underestimated. Take Moses, the Jewish lawgiver *par excellence*. God charged him with leading his people out of Egypt (Exodus 4: 2–4). But Moses feared that the people would not believe he had spoken to the Lord:

> And the Lord said unto him, What is that in thine hand? And he said, A rod.
>
> And he said, Cast it on the ground. And he cast it on the ground, and it became a serpent; and Moses fled from before it.
>
> And the Lord said unto Moses, Put forth thine hand, and take it by the tail. And he put forth his hand and caught it, and it became a rod in his hand.
>
> That they may believe that the Lord God of their fathers, the God of Abraham, the God of Isaac, and the God of Jacob, hath appeared unto thee.

Gustave Doré, *Moses and Aaron before Pharaoh*, an illustration to *Exodus* (1865)

Accompanied by Aaron, Moses performed this feat at Pharaoh's court. When Pharaoh ordered his magicians to repeat it, all their rods were turned into serpents. Aaron's rod then swallowed them up, and he emerged as the victor of the contest (Exodus 7: 10–12). Because Pharaoh remained unconvinced, Moses called up the seven plagues with his rod. Thus he had the frogs come out of the Nile to smite the entire land of Egypt. In a sense, Moses was the very opposite of a fakir.

A snake charmer can cause a serpent to turn as stiff as a rod; when he suddenly seizes the snake it goes quite limp again. But here the very opposite happened. The true legislator is able to pass off a piece of wood as a snake . . . To render the unfamiliar (God) familiar, he renders the familiar (the rod) unfamiliar.

THE AESTHETIC OF THE EMPTY GESTURE

The trick with the rod and the serpent illustrates the true cunning of the legislator: to render the unnatural social contract acceptable, he alienates man from his natural egoism. 'He must, in a word, take away from man his own resources and give him instead new ones alien to him.' He is able to transform natural power into political power. By virtue of the social contract, the individualism that stands in the way of unity is suddenly converted into the basis of society: for selfish reasons men pursue the common good. What we have here is an aesthetic of the empty gesture; a trifling difference makes a world of difference. Thanks to the social contract, man is suddenly changed from a dumb animal into a thinking being. Impulse becomes duty. Instinct becomes justice. What men have surrendered as individuals they regain as citizens. Democracy is a gift man gives to himself.

THE HOLY DEMOCRAT

However, here we come up against a paradox. The legislator himself seems to stand outside the democratic society he champions. After all, he has not been brought in by the people, but has appointed himself. Moreover he seems to lack all human attributes. To exclude any suspicion of self-interest, the legislator must resign from all his offices. He must set to work like a stranger in his own land, forfeit glory and power, be devoid of all passion. Rousseau presents him as a kind of saint.

The joke is that the definition Rousseau gives of the godlike outsider fits the democratic subject to perfection. Formal democracy is anti-humanist, not fashioned in the image of man with his passions, interests and needs, but in that of a cold abstraction. Democracy embraces all men, 'regardless of person', irrespective of race, religion, wealth and other follies.

The true democrat is of course a Utopian figure; behind every citizen stands a calculating bourgeois in pursuit of his own interests. But that is no problem because the bourgeois becomes a bourgeois by his attempt to behave like a bourgeois, regardless of his selfish motives. The democratic subject, in short, coincides with his own shortcomings. Democracy succeeds through failure.

And there lies the explanation of the exceptional position of the mythical legislator. He patently embodies an unattainable ideal. Precisely as a super-democrat he seems to stand outside the democracy he proclaims. But on closer inspection, the super-bourgeois in his absurdity renders tangible the Utopian character of the Utopia he preaches, the fictional character of his fiction. He embodies the stupidity of democracy, the stupidity that defines democracy. The legislator is a part of the myth he proclaims.

The legislator is not democratically elected, but according to Rousseau is retrospectively appointed leader by the nation he himself has founded. He is an arbitrary idiot who knows how to write himself into the story after the event: success legitimizes his high-handed action.

THE WOLF IN SHEEP'S CLOTHING

Rousseau distinguishes between the 'general will', which aims to preserve society and freedom within it, and the 'will of all', the sum of all forms of self-interest. Politics has the impossible task of squaring the circle: of reconciling the will of all with the general will.

The starting-point of the democratic decision process is the majority principle. But, during elections society breaks up into a loose collection of individuals, each in pursuit of his own self-interest. Only by accident is the will of all identical with the general will. Unanimity, however, is no guarantee of political sense, which demands that every voter keep the general interest in mind.

Now this poses a problem: 'The individuals see the good they reject; the public wills the good but it does not see.' According to Rousseau, individuals are not stupid, but bad. The people as a whole, by contrast, are not bad but stupid, a prey to fraud by special interest groups (one reason why Rousseau was opposed to political parties). This is reminiscent of our earlier distinction between savageness ('*Wildheit*') and roughness ('*Roheit*').

It is the task of politicians to tame the wily wolf and to enlighten the stupid sheep. The joke is of course that wolf and sheep are found in one and the same human being. Tension between the private and the public sphere defines the democrat. Strictly speaking, the social contract is a pact man signs with himself: an obligation the citizen as a member of the collective enters into with himself as a private person. But ultimately that action is also inspired by self-interest. Man always remains a wolf in sheep's clothing.

In general, too, the private sphere cannot be separated from the public domain. Society cannot prosper if its people do not prosper; however, the well-being of each individual separately does not necessarily lead to the well-being of the state. It is the tension between the part and the whole that keeps the engine running.

Paradoxically, the best guarantee of general prosperity is the greatest possible difference between private interests. The greater the differences are, the more general will be the outcome of the ballot. Unity is promoted by the greatest possible discord.

THE STRENGTH OF DEMOCRACY

The will of the people is the guiding principle used in the promulgation of laws. But how can that will be determined? In a democracy, no one is above the parties. There is no point from which the general interest can be assessed. Even the legislators are subject to the law. The legitimacy of the law is a constant subject of a discussion that renders a definite determination of the will of the people impossible.

This weakness is at one and the same time the strength of democracy. Democracy flourishes precisely in the clamour both for and against, in the unceasing debate about what the will of the people really is. In a democracy the conflict is institutionalized. Every solution is temporary. Democracy is nothing but the product of a series of Boeotian attempts to come to grips with democracy.

THE PARADOX OF DEMOCRACY

Democracy means government by the people. But what is a people if not a collection of subjects? The people cannot be ruler and subject at the same time. Thus the people themselves stand in the way of becoming a people. That is the folly of democracy.

This paradox is highlighted during the most democratic of processes: in the course of elections, whose aim is to determine the will of people, the social structure disintegrates into a collection of asocial idiots. Elections are not about the quality of the individual voters, but about a purely quantitative procedure, the counting of votes. The citizen is reduced to an element of a purely numerical set. In short, at the moment the people actually hold power, they cease to exist as a unit.

ELECTIONS

For a state in which the law is respected, democracy is the worst possible form of government, but if the law is not respected, it is the best of all.
Plato, *Politicus*

Democracy is the worst form of government except all those other forms that have been tried from time to time.
Sir Winston Churchill

During elections, reason is hard to find. You have only to think of the influence of the weather on the outcome: the better the weather, the more votes are cast, and the better it is for the Left. Leftist voters are fair-weather voters. But this only holds true in those countries that have bad weather conditions . . . Oddly enough, this aspect has been ignored in the writings of Montesquieu, Grotius, Rousseau and others about the influence of climatic conditions on the choice of government.

The candidates act out of self-interest. They are after power, money or the satisfaction of their particular form of idealism. Beyond that, they pull out every possible rhetorical stop, playing on the voters' fears, frustrations and avarice, in short on their emotions.

The voters are not much better. They allow themselves to be swayed by their individual, selfish, anarchist rather than democratic views. Moreover, they are prey to their emotions. They are open to demagogy and to all sorts of provocation. An unforeseen or carefully staged event, for instance a scandal shortly before the elections, can determine the future of the country. And who, outside the professional political circus, still takes notice of party programmes?

Those citizens who nevertheless vote out of a democratic sense of duty are looked on as mugs by the rest. Worse still, these nitpickers may even pose a threat to democracy. Those who want to rationalize democracy, to subject voters to an intelligence test before they are allowed to cast their vote, are in pursuit of a dictatorship of the intellect. If, before an election, we were to dredge up the past of the candidates, if we were to test all citizens for their grasp of politics, we would end up with a democracy run on the model of the former socialist republics, where the actual elections were held before the official poll.

Idiocy is no argument against democracy. Far from it: democracy exists by the grace of idiocy. The quest for complete rationality results in anti-democratic measures. Democracy only succeeds in failure, in vain attempts to be a pure democracy. But all this happens behind the scenes. That is why we pretend that elections are the apex of democracy.

Democracy is a fiction. In reality only asocial idiots exist. However, without the fiction of democracy, real democracy could not survive. Democracy is the semblance of democracy.

Stupidity reigns supreme once everyone truly believes that democracy exists and that elections are its climax.

THE ELECTION MACHINE

The paradoxical nature of democracy is highlighted in Isaac Asimov's *Franchise*, a science fiction story published in 1955. In some distant future, an old man explains that everybody used to vote under the old American electoral system. Those who received the most votes were elected. However, because voting took too long, machines were invented to look at the first few votes and compare them with the votes from the same places in previous years and thence to predict the final result.

The machines kept growing bigger and needed fewer and fewer votes; in the end a single vote was enough for the new-built Multivac machine to predict the outcome of all local and national elections. 'Multivac weighs all sorts of known factors, billions of them. One factor isn't known, though. [. . .] That's the reaction pattern of the human mind.'

In short, what cannot be rationalized are the American people, the *raison d'être* of American democracy. Still, through an arbitrarily chosen citizen, Multivac can arrive at the thoughts of all other Americans. Thus Norman Muller, an ordinary clerk in a small department store in Bloomington, Indiana, was chosen by Multivac as Voter of the Year:

> Multivac has picked you as most representative this year. Not the smartest, or the strongest, or the luckiest, but just the most representative. Now we don't question Multivac, do we?

But Norman does not want to shoulder the responsibility. 'Why me?' His wife, Sarah tries to reassure him: 'Multivac has picked you. It's Multivac's responsibility. Everyone knows that.' Nevertheless this one voter is held responsible for the election of the President, and also for the President's possible failings. Much like the truck farmer Humphrey MacComber, 'who didn't ask to be picked. Why was it [the recent administration] his fault more than anyone else? Now his name is a curse.' Sarah tells Norman that his new status might earn him fame and money. 'That's not the point in being a Voter, Sarah.' 'That will be your point.'

To prevent politicians, salesmen and cranks from influencing him, Norman is not allowed to leave the house until election day. Newspapers and TV are forbidden, so that he can face Multivac 'in as normal a state of mind as possible'.

The polling booth appears to have been installed in a hospital. 'We want you to stay with us all day if necessary, just so that you get used to your surroundings and get over any thought you might have that there is anything unusual in this, anything clinical, if you know what I mean.' Norman's body is attached to some 'formidable' machinery, which records his blood pressure, heartbeat, skin conductivity and brain-wave pattern. 'You won't even know it's going on.' The doctors emphasize that the machine is not a lie detector, it is simply a piece of technology designed to establish how intensely Norman is affected by the questions put to him. 'It will understand your feelings better than you yourself.' The Multivac machine, which, incidentally, he never sees, asks him incongruous and banal questions: 'What do you think of the price of eggs?'

Avarice persuades Norman to do his duty and to act like a democrat. But suddenly something other than personal gain starts to enter his thoughts:

> A latent patriotism was stirring. After all, he was representing the entire electorate. He was the focal point for them. He was, in his own person, for this one day, all of America! [...]
> Suddenly, Norman Muller felt proud. It was on him now in full strength. He was proud.
> In this imperfect world, the sovereign citizens of the first and greatest Electronic Democracy had, through Norman Muller (through him!), exercised once again their free, untrammeled franchise.

Asimov's story is not so much a caricature of democracy as an imitation of the insanity lurking at its heart.

In the attempt to rationalize democracy, the machine cannot dispense with the voter. The voter is the lunatic element of democracy. But by confining itself to just one voter, the machine puts an end to party political strife; moreover, the sole voter stops the people from becoming estranged from what is an uncaring state apparatus. Thanks to Norman, democracy is given a human face. His name becomes a synonym for the success or failure of the President. In short, the irony is that the voter is held responsible for the election result. Thus the machine comes out top. The voter becomes the alibi for the elusive state apparatus, which owes its authority to the citizens' fears.

To limit the risks, Multivac elects the elector. But Norman's role is purely formal. He has nothing to say. The machine leaves him, however, with the delusion that his vote is essential. For that reason, the story may also be read as an illustration of the fantasy that the individual vote decides the outcome of an election, and not the sum of all the votes. The citizen votes as if the entire weight of democracy rests on his shoulders. During elections, every citizen thinks he is a prince.

The special status every elector arrogates to himself is put into proper perspective by the explanation of the election of the Elector of the Year. Norman is presented as the American *par excellence*. This seems an impossible role – small wonder that Norman is struck dumb. What does he have that others do not have? Paradoxically, Norman is distinguished by what most Americans have in common. Multivac relies on the norm in Norman. His originality lies in the fact that he is the least original citizen, that he is abnormally normal, unique in his banality. Because he is anything but a special human being, he is the American citizen *par excellence*.

The normal democratic subject is not the most intelligent but the most average person. The whole system revolves around a single idiot who represents the rest of the electorate in his mediocrity. The 'average American' is of course a figment of the imagination; the average person, for instance, has 1.3 children. Like all extremes, the average, too, is an ideal to which no individual measures up, not even Norman. But his stock reactions to his role make him the ideal candidate. By his selfish doubts, Norman becomes the embodiment of the common denominator. In this one citizen the sovereign American people encounters itself as a bigoted asocial creature.

Though the typical American cannot be clinically investigated by Multivac, the struggle of a random subject to come to terms with his role can. That also emerges from the perverse instruction by the doctors when they tell Norman to behave normally. Strictly speaking, Norman's intellect cannot be measured, but Norman's reactions to the impossible task of being himself can be analysed. It is precisely the fears and the uncertainty Norman feels about his identity that constitute the measurable core of his being.

In the end, Norman begins to believe in his task, and in so doing satisfies the definition of the true citizen, albeit in retrospect.

ELECTION MADNESS

Though a Leftist or Rightist radical may do violence to the democratic norms, he does not shake the foundations of democracy. Elections, by contrast, pose a direct threat to democracy because they are not a rebellion but a lawful democratic revolt against democracy. The people normally subjected to the will of legislators are suddenly set above the legislators, opening up an abyss in which the established order disappears. Elections mean not only the end of those temporarily in charge of the country, but also the suicide of democracy.

Yet, once this round of self-destruction is over, once the serpent has swallowed itself, a new order emerges.

Seen in that light, every democracy is a caricature of itself – anarchy becomes democracy. Democracy has its roots in a self-denying, legitimized idiocy.

This self-destructive aspect has to be concealed if democracy is to keep its credibility. Stupidity only works unseen. Yet stupidity must never be ignored, because it constitutes the very basis of democracy. For that reason the pathological self-destruction constituting the reverse of unselfish self-sacrifice must be allowed to surface from time to time.

Democracy proves its strength by leaving the voters free to give vent to their idiocy during elections. Only the will to stupidity, the will to surrender to irrational chance, renders democracy possible.

However there is always the risk that elections may degenerate into anarchy and thus put a final end to democracy. For that reason the centre of power, which is the centre of idiocy, may not be left vacant for too long.

But democracy is threatened by yet another danger.

THE CENTRE OF POWER

> Brekeke-kesh, koash, koash
> Brekeke-kesh, koash, koash.
> Aristophanes, *The Frogs*

Democracy is based on the belief that those elected by the people for their desirable qualities will govern the country rationally. But who judges the qualities of those who judge the qualities? There is no ultimate guarantee of the suitability of the rulers.

The representatives of the people in a democracy can never dominate the political order because they remain subjects, they are judged by others. In short, democracy is defined by an insuperable barrier preventing subjects from occupying the centre of power for good. Democracy is a permanent transition, a continuous interregnum. The acceptance of this immanent impossibility is characteristic of democracy. The election result entitles a subject to hold power temporarily, as a stand-in for an impossible ruler. He has the status of a plenipotentiary. (Claude Lefort, *L'Invention démocratique*, Paris, 1981)

Lest ministers grow too attached to their plush armchairs, we refer disdainfully to government money-grubbers, metropolitan arrogance, big shots, and so forth. In that way we remind ourselves and those who govern us of the distance between them and the centre of power.

Because nobody can be a direct embodiment of the people, the locus of power must remain vacant. Our temporary rulers occupy no more than the empty seat of an impossible sovereignty.

The centre of power is a purely symbolic place; a holder of real political power cannot occupy it without transforming democracy into a dictatorship. Successful politicians pose the greatest danger to democracy.

THE TERROR

> We must strive for democracy – and prevent its realization.
> Robert Musil, *Tagebücher*

The paradox of democracy was caricatured by the Jacobins during the French Revolution. The Terror was based on the fantasy of the radical destruction of the feudal system, and the creation of the New Man *ex nihilo*. That this was no more than a pipedream is borne out by a circular argument: the People charges the National Convention (comprising the People's representatives) to bring the People into being. This fantasy disguises the fact that the state is not the product of a rational decision, but of irrational forces. No one knew this better than the Jacobins.

The legitimacy of the terror was proclaimed by Saint-Just: 'No one can govern innocently.' Everyone who rules on behalf of the people

Robespierre guillotining the executioner after having guillotined all the French, 1794

The criminal obverse of the law is expressed in the joke: 'Are there any executioners left? No, we cut off the head of the last one yesterday.' Robespierre, too, ended up under the guillotine.

must needs dirty his hands. 'The Terror is revolutionary inasmuch as it stops anyone from occupying the centre of power; and in that sense it has a democratic character' (Charles Lefort). That is also the reason why many preferred to lose their heads rather than take part in the Terror. 'We are not virtuous enough to be so terrible' (Saint-Just). The Jacobins were afraid that, while wielding terror in the service of the people, they might themselves be swayed by covert self-interest.

But the joke is that the position from which the Jacobins managed to stop the centre of power from being occupied was itself the centre of absolute power. No one can escape. Sooner or later, the Jacobins' heads, too, would roll under the guillotine. The hero of the Revolution is by definition a traitor because he differs from the rest. Hence the vicious circle of the Terror: an untold number of democrats who cut off one another's heads. The Revolution was a snake devouring its own children, and ultimately itself as well.

STUPOR

Every political order is familiar with the totalitarian temptation. But the quest for complete rationality is sapped by a form of idiocy against which every form of organization comes up sooner or later, an incomprehensible idiocy threatening to reduce the whole system to caricature. On the one hand, idiocy may prove fatal to democracy: there is the danger that elections may degenerate into anarchy and so put a final end to democratic rule. The centre of power may not remain vacant for too long.

On the other hand, democracy cannot manage without idiocy. There is the other danger that someone may seize the centre of power and cause the political order to degenerate into a stifling dictatorship.

In brief, democracy is threatened by panic and dullness, two forms of stupor, a term etymologically related to 'stupidity'. Too much idiocy leads to folly, too little to stupefaction. In other words, idiocy must be kept at bay even while it is embraced.

How can we breach this dilemma of democracy? By deliberately allowing for stupidity. Here, constitutional monarchy provides the solution.

I THE LOG IN THE LAKE

Democracy can only be achieved with the help of a single subject who embodies the absurdity of democracy, namely a king. The monarch does not merely personify the people but is able to forge them into a society by embodying the impossible idea of the People as a whole. The absurdity of the king renders tangible the stupidity of the democratic state that revolves around him, the failure without which democracy cannot succeed.

The coronation of a monarch does not fill the vacuum of power. Anomalously, the monarch keeps free the space in which democracy can arise. Unlike the Jacobin who occupies the centre of power by keeping it vacant, the monarch protects the empty space by occupying it.

The king prevents politicians from growing too accustomed to their plush armchairs. Since the function of the monarch is purely negative, his qualities do not matter, and the question of who is fit to be monarch must be left to the accident of natural selection and

Gustave Doré, *The Frogs who Wanted a King*

reproduction. Only in that way is the futility of his person made manifest.

II THE SANCTIFIED SPACE

The monarch is by definition a cheat, someone who lands in the empty locus of power by chance, and goes on to act as if he embodied the elusive People. In fact, the monarch embodies the distance between the locus of power and those who wield it. He owes his fascinating authority not to his qualities, but to the fact that he occupies a sanctified space in the democratic order.

To put an end to his charisma, we must expose the gap between the monarch and this void. The exposure puts an end to the monarch's power, but not to the vacant space he occupies. This void cannot be remedied because it is a structural necessity, reflecting the immanent folly of democracy.

Kamagurka, cartoon in *Vrij Nederland*.
The emperor's clothes do not hide his naked body, but the vacant centre of power

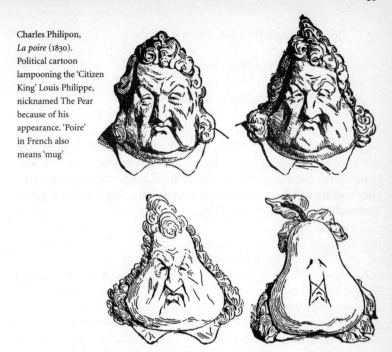

Charles Philipon, *La poire* (1830). Political cartoon lampooning the 'Citizen King' Louis Philippe, nicknamed The Pear because of his appearance. 'Poire' in French also means 'mug'

III ELBOW ROOM

Quoi, Quoi? Dis donc pourquoi?
(What, what? Say why?)
Jean-Philippe Rameau, *Platée*

On the one hand the monarch prevents politicians from wielding permanent power; on the other, he guarantees the continued existence of democracy during elections. (That the opposite is also possible was demonstrated in Belgium, when the king abdicated temporarily to avoid signing in new abortion laws, and democracy guaranteed the continuity of the monarchy.)

Without a monarch, the political order may degenerate into anarchy in which no one is certain of his place, or into a dictatorship in which everyone is assigned a fixed position and role. The monarch opens the space in which citizens can become themselves without unleashing a war of all against all.

IV THE SUBJECT OF DEMOCRACY

Render unto Caesar the things which are Caesar's. As a subject, an obedient citizen of the State, you must unconditionally act as if the monarch embodied the law, to acquire the freedom to prove yourself a subject in the other meaning of the word – a critical individual who questions all authority.

The paradox is that citizens only gain their freedom by subjecting themselves to a person onto whom they have projected their free will, namely the head of state. The contradiction is inherent in the very word 'subject', which means a subordinate as well as someone with a free will; the subject can only exist in voluntary slavery.

V THE BODY POLITIC

Citizens are routinely confronted by the shadowy state apparatus that shapes their lives behind their backs. Subjects overcome their alienation by acting as if the monarch were the state incarnate.

The monarch adds the subjective 'I will' to the objective law, and transforms the opinion of ministers into government decrees. With his signature he turns laws into the expression of his personal will. This is also the logic of such empty gestures as cutting ribbons, kissing babies, and laying foundation stones.

Yet as soon as the monarch meddles with the contents of the law, he crosses the boundary that separates him from his subjects. The state loses its human face and becomes a stifling dictatorship.

VI 'A MIRROR FOR PRINCES'

They want me for a constitutional monarch, like those pagan gods who *os habent et non loquuntur; pedes habent et non ambulant* (who have mouths and do not speak, who have feet and do not walk).

William I, King of the Netherlands, to a delegation asking him to grant them ministerial responsibility, 1829

Common sense tells us that a monarch should be as wise, able and

Pim van Boxsel, *Constitutional Monarchy* (1969)

brave as possible. The opposite is true. The gulf between his symbolic role and his actual talents can never be wide enough. The major threat to democracy is precisely the coincidence of the role and the person of the monarch, and the illusion that his authority is founded on reason. The log would be transformed into a snake.

The relationship between task and talent also distinguishes the monarch from his ministers. The ministers are chosen for their ability. They apply the concrete contents of the law. The king, by contrast, has a purely ceremonial role. He freely accepts the inevitable. All he has to do is to append his signature. But then, his is the last word. He rules in name only, but in that name rests his authority.

Because it concerns a foolish, purely formal act, the role of head of state can be vested in an idiot who has reached his position on such an irrational ground as birth. The monarch holds an exceptional position in the state apparatus, one in which it matters little whether he is stupid or not. It is even a reassuring thought that the former Dutch queen, Juliana, the Belgian heir apparent, Albert, and Charles, Prince of Wales, consult visitors from outer-space, trees and dolphins. The constitutional monarchy is a rational unit with an irrational element at its head. The gulf between People and king is no impediment to, but a prerequisite of, democracy. The political order needs an exceptional focus, a force willing to assume responsibility and to render that order effective.

The objection of republican critics to monarchy, namely that the fate of the state hinges on the accidental character traits of the monarch, is futile; since his authority is purely formal, his qualities are irrelevant.

A president, by contrast, poses a threat to democracy: there is a good chance that we come to believe in his rationality. A king at least is manifestly out of place.

As if to avoid misunderstandings, many French presidents have behaved like monarchs, as witness their rhetoric, triumphal arches and palaces of art. In other respects, too, political leaders emphasize their irrationality. Not only Hitler and Stalin, but also Churchill, Reagan and Mitterand consulted astrologers.

VII PINOCCHIO

Centuries ago there lived – 'A king!' my little readers will say immediately. No, children, you are mistaken. Once upon a time there was a piece of wood.

Carlo Collodi, *The Adventures of Pinocchio* (1881)

Pinocchio is a ne'er-do-well. He is a 'wooden' and heartless boy, and does not honour his parents. As the tale unfolds, however, he gradually begins to show signs of humanity. Whenever he tells lies, his nose grows longer, which suggests that he has a conscience. But only after he has shown that he has a sense of duty and genuine feelings, such as love, does he change into a boy of flesh and blood. On a chair beside him he discovers the inert wooden puppet that he once was.

This fairy-tale illustrates the ideal course of development of a constitutional monarch. To prevent a clash between his symbolic role and his qualities, the monarch has to start out as a lump of wood. Subsequently he must develop the ability to distinguish between himself as a private and as a public figure. The monarch must be shrewd enough to behave like a fool. At public appearances he must conduct himself like a puppet, a dry old stick, making it clear that he is playing a part. He must not show any genuine feelings, or honour his parents other than formally. The ultimate proof of his fitness is the involuntary expression of a sense of shame. To prevent his nose from becoming too conspicuous, he must keep his public appearances as brief as possible.

VIII FAILURE AS A *RATIO COGNOSCENDI*

Preserve us from clever kings! Charles i had his head chopped
off, Charles ii sold his country to the French. Don't think so
much! If you're not happy, then renounce the throne.
Advice by a British tabloid newspaper to Charles, Prince of Wales

The monarch is the only person who does not have to prove himself, because he is by nature what he is by culture. His social position is defined by a biological fact: he is king by birth.

His subjects, by contrast, lack a genealogy. They are orphaned, worth only what they make of themselves. They have to prove themselves. Failure, the discrepancy between what they do and what they ought to be, is precisely what enables us to assess their merit.

Furthermore, we only become aware of our democratic duties through the realization that we have failed to fulfil them. We would otherwise be acting as puppets and not as free subjects. Failure is the *ratio cognoscendi* of democracy.

The monarch, for his part, cannot and must not be judged by his qualities, lest his authority be undermined. Had the monarch constantly to prove himself, he would become a subject of the sovereign people. For that reason, too, the decision as to who stands at the head of the people must be left to the irrational, biological fact of lineage. The monarch is a success by birth. His actions cannot be gauged by an ideal, by what he ought to be doing, because the monarch is the ideal by nature. He cannot break the law because his word is law. He is what he symbolizes. Or rather, no matter what he does, his subjects are obliged to act as if he embodied the law.

The greatest threat to the authority of the monarch, however, is posed by enthusiastic supporters who try to prove how wise a ruler he is, the better to justify his position. Those who obey the monarch, not because he is king, but because he is a man of genius or an outstanding leader, are guilty of lese-majesty. They set themselves above the

monarch. They undermine his authority, which is based on blind
obedience and not on rational arguments.

IX I WILL

The monarch's decisions are not based on the law. He derives his
authority from a free, untrammelled decision. The monarch 'wills'
a particular law, not because it is good; a law is good because the
monarch wills it so. He does not follow the light of reason, but his
arbitrary will. He knows what he wants but cannot explain why,
even if he were asked to do so. Unaccountable folly is the monarch's
prerogative. And it works, as long as his decision is purely formal.

The enforcement of the monarch's will is a violation of the democratic process sanctioned by the constitution. The monarch, who is
subject to democratic law, temporarily becomes an absolute ruler,
the free subject *par excellence*. His inherently feudal action formally
puts an end to the incessant clamour for and against the law. The
implementation of his will undermines the sovereignty of the People,
but at one and the same time underpins the new law. Democracy
cannot dispense with the monarch's consent.

X THE POINT OF FOLLY

The king is democracy's centre of folly. He fascinates us not by his
outlandishness but because he reminds us of the hidden side of democracy: the asocial, self-destructive freedom that stands in the way of
unity even while constituting its basis.

The monarch does not express the will of the nation. He is able to
achieve national unity by embodying the egoistic folly that stands in
the way of unity. It is precisely the imperfect nature of the monarch (in
the eyes of democrats), the point at which the constitutional monarch
displays absolutist traits, which appeals to the imagination. As an
obstacle, the king is a reminder of the fact that democracy is the con-
gealed form of an original folly that can re-emerge at any moment. The
citizens are united by their fascination with an authoritarian subject
who gives tangible proof of the immanent impossibility of national
unity. By reminding the nation through his idiocy of the shaky

foundations of democracy, he keeps order. Without the monarch, the state would disintegrate.

Democracy exists solely in the series of vain attempts to come to terms with the idiocy vested in the monarch. In him, we celebrate the stupidity of democracy.

XI *L'ÉTAT C'EST MOI*

The monarch does not represent an order inherent in mankind; he creates order out of nothing. He is a symbol to which the symbolized content owes its existence. The monarch is no sage who grasps all the possibilities present in the nation, but someone who is able, by a completely irrational gesture, to transform the formless mass into a rational whole.

The monarch is thus not merely a symbol of the community, an aesthetic appendage, the 'crowning touch', but embodies the state in a non-symbolic way: the monarch in his irrational presence is the rational state. In his body, the state attains its purpose.

The fascinating presence of the monarch blinds us to the bureaucratic apparatus that structures the prevailing order. Nor is that all: bureaucracy can only fulfil its purpose with the help of an idiot, by the irrational presence of the monarch. Order is bound up indissolubly with a single subject who, in his idiocy, happens to be that order.

Without a king, no democracy. Unity is always a unity of opposites. A rational order can only exist if it is embodied in the irrational figure of the monarch. The central figure, thanks to whom the nation attains its unity and identity, coincides with the point that stands in the way of democracy.

Precisely because he is an idiot who is alien to democracy, who has no equal, the monarch saves democracy. However, his subjects necessarily ignore the fact that their existence is closely bound up with this egregious idiot; they look upon themselves as the essence of democracy, and consider the monarch a bizarre, folkloristic appendage.

XII *STUPOR MUNDI*

There is but one step from the sublime to the ridiculous.

Attributed to Napoleon I, on his retreat from Russia, 1812
(after Thomas Paine, *The Age of Reason*, 1795)

The monarch is an offence against the democratic principle by which
all citizens are considered equal. The reduction of democracy to a king
is beyond the republican's powers of imagination, and evokes the
stupefaction that defines the true democrat.

On the one hand, the king prevents total democracy; on the other
he conveys a negative impression of what a true democracy might be
like. The joke is, of course, that democracy does not exist outside the
vain attempt to bring it about. That is why we have to see both
aspects in a single context: in his absurdity, the monarch embodies
the failure that democracy is in essence. Seen in that light, the sublime ruler is a ridiculous fool, a lump of wood occupying the vacant
seat of democracy.

It will not do to object that no one is a true democrat. This argument suggests that a faultless democrat is a possibility. In fact, the true
democrat exists only in his vain attempts to be a true democrat. And
in his idiocy, the monarch materializes that impossibility. The secret of
the monarch lies in the failure of democracy.

6 THE EMPEROR'S NEW CLOTHES

ESSE EST NON PERCIPI

The non-awareness of reality is part of its essence.

Alfred Sohn-Rehel, *Geistige und körperliche Arbeit* (1972)

The world exists by virtue of a stupidity that, by definition, works only when it goes undetected. Misjudgement, in short, is productive. The existence of the world implies a non-knowing: *esse est non percipi*.

The illusion is twofold: it does not so much blind us to reality; self-evident reality exists by virtue of an illusion that structures reality so long as it is not perceived.

In short, in the world we take for granted, we overlook the illusion and the idiocy residing in it. Disclosure of the illusion implies exposure of the idiocy.

Democracy can only work if we are blind to its truth, that is to its antagonistic forces. The failure to grasp the true nature of democracy is part of democracy itself. As soon as we see the real state of affairs, our world collapses. Illusion is thus inherent in the essence of that world. There is no constitutional monarchy without mystification. Appearances control the political order.

HOW TILL EULENSPIEGEL PAINTED THE LANDGRAVE OF HESSE

The Landgrave of Hesse ordered Till Eulenspiegel to fill the great hall of his castle with paintings of the 'lords and landgraves of Hessian blood together with their ladies'. Till was further instructed to depict the way in which the Landgrave's forefathers were related to the kings of Hungary and various princes.

*Till Eulenspiegel with the
Landgrave of Hesse*

An early woodcut

Till and his merry men passed their time squandering the advance they had been given of 100 guilders. After a while the Landgrave asked to see how the work was progressing. Till warned him that 'whosoever is born out of wedlock will be unable to see my painting', then pulled aside a white cloth that had been hung across the wall. Using a short white staff, he began to point out members of the Landgrave's family, going as far back as his Roman ancestors.

The Landgrave thought to himself, I must be the son of a whore for I can see nothing but a white wall. But he said, 'Master, your work is greatly pleasing to us, but we lack the skill to fathom its deeper meaning.'

The Landgrave decided to return with all his knights to discover which of them was born out of wedlock, since in such a case his fief would revert to the Landgrave.

Meanwhile his wife, accompanied by eight maidens and a female jester, inspected the artist's work. Not one of them could see anything, but they all kept their counsel. Finally the jester said, 'I can't see any painting, even if I am called illegitimate for the rest of my life!' Then Till Eulenspiegel thought to himself, When fools begin speaking the truth, it's high time I made myself scarce.

Till did not deceive the people by painting a completely invented genealogy. He set to work in a more subtle way. He deceived them by pretending that the secret of power lay hidden behind a white cloth, when the cloth covered nothing at all. In fact, he was speaking the truth: behind the curtain we discover that deception is the secret foundation of power. This is what has to be kept secret if the political order is not to fall apart. Appearances are the essence! That is the genealogy, or rather the anti-genealogy of power. The truth of power lies not *behind*, but *in* the curtain. The essence does not exist outside the cloth, which purports to be no more than a curtain.

The cloth appears to hide the fact that there is nothing to hide. Behind the curtain there is nothing to see, but we have to discover this nothing as such: behind the curtain the possibility of illusion lies hidden. The curtain allows for projections, and that is why it cannot be removed without punishment.

What Till exposes is not only that there is nothing to see. Behind the curtain, the Landgrave's subjects discover that the secret of power lies in their own fascination, in their stupefaction at the sublime person of the prince: *stupor mundi*. In short, what the citizens encounter behind the curtain is themselves. But the discovery that they themselves constitute the basis of power is fatal. (Compare this with the professional cyclist who reaches his limit and collapses. The realization that the winner's medal was the pretext for wrestling with himself would be crippling.)

The disclosure of the basis of regal power puts an end not only to illusion and ignorance, but also to the order built upon them. In the nature of things, stupidity only works when it goes unseen. *Esse est non percipi.*

THE MONARCH'S TWO BODIES

The monarch owes his charisma to a stupid custom, to a symbolic rite. This constitutes the mystical basis of his authority. To rid ourselves of the monarch we need merely abolish the established order. As soon as the mechanism behind the monarch's charismatic authority is unmasked, he loses his power. We discern the empty, ceremonial nature of his role and the banality of his person. Not being condemned to death, but being treated as an equal by his subjects is the greatest punishment for a king.

> I do not ask you to overthrow him or cause him to totter, but simply that you cease to prop him up. Then you will see him collapse like some colossus, stripped of his pedestal, and buried under his own weight.

The distinction Etienne de la Boétie draws in his *Discours de la servitude volontaire* (*c.* 1550) between the symbolic role of the king and his person ignores a remarkable phenomenon. The symbolic role splits the monarch's body into a visible, transitory body and another, intangible, one. Not only has the monarch's tangible body suddenly become the bearer of sublime body, but if we treat the monarch long enough as a monarch, then his everyday qualities undergo a transubstantiation and become the cause of amazement, of stupor. (Ernst Kantorowicz, *The King's Two Bodies*, Princeton, 1957)

Thanks to its vulnerability, the king's body exerts a fascination, and acts as mediator between the human and the divine. And the more the king acts like the man in the street, embroiled in idiotic everyday emotions, the more of a king he becomes. For that reason, mockery, far from posing a threat to his power, only serves to strengthen it. Even regicide does not put an end to the king's mystical body. Why does this exalted body appear? Whence this fascination?

VOLUNTARY SLAVERY

> He who rules over you has but two eyes, two hands, one body, and nothing that the meanest citizen from the infinitely great number in your towns lacks, save for the advantage you give him, namely the power to destroy you. Where would he come by enough eyes with which to spy on you, had you not given them to him?
>
> Etienne de la Boétie, *Discours de la servitude volontaire* (*c.* 1550)

To rid ourselves of a monarch we need only cease treating him like one – 'not by an act of liberation, but simply by expressing the will to be free'. Whosoever wants freedom can have it; wish and fulfilment are one and the same thing. However, men do not want freedom. And for no other reason, it seems to me, than that they could have it if they wanted it. It is as if they refused to seize that great good simply because it is too easy.

We desire desire, not its fulfilment. Fulfilment stands in the way of desire. That explains why the king's subjects are embroiled in the paradox of voluntary slavery. And similarly, the relationship between monarch and democracy is elucidated.

The sublime king whose will is law, who curbs our 'ruthless quest for freedom', is a ruse to save democracy. In the fantasy figure of the king who stands in the way of democracy, we externalize the im-manent failure of that system. The king prevents a democracy, which is structurally impossible. Thus we preserve the illusion that without this obstacle, we should be completely free. Meanwhile we dismiss any idea of getting rid of the king, because that would expose the fiction of national unity. It is precisely as a figure that cannot be integrated into social life that the monarch guarantees democracy. Democracy only flourishes in the contrast between the masses and the one subject who embodies the impossibility of the democratic order.

His mystical body is not a palpable proof of the immortal identity of the nation, but of the essential failure that defines democracy. His fascinating body is 'something of nothing', the negativity of democracy materialized.

Voluntary slavery is a way of saving desire. The will to power, by contrast, peters out.

THE JUSTIFICATION

The secret of the royal palace is that there is no secret.

As subjects we are necessarily victims of the illusion that the monarch is a monarch *tout court*. The realization that his power rests on blind adoration would not only put an end to that power, but also to the nation ruled by him. That is why the monarch legitimizes his power with an appeal, not to democracy, but to an external authority: God or a mystical past. In time, everyone begins to believe him.

But does this still apply in the age of the end of ideologies?

THE EMPEROR'S NEW CLOTHES

The working principle of constitutional monarchies is beautifully illustrated in Hans Christian Andersen's fairy-tale, 'The Emperor's New Clothes'. One day two rogues, calling themselves weavers, claimed that they knew how to make linen so fine it was invisible to anyone unfit for the office he held, and to simpletons. Because the emperor wanted to know which of his ministers were foolish or unfit for office, he ordered himself new clothes.

The joke is of course that this linen did not exist, and that the emperor was naked. But everybody, the emperor included, acted as if he were fully dressed, because nobody wanted to be taken for a fool.

Here we have the logic of constitutional monarchy. It is based on the concealment of an idiocy: the monarch becomes royal because we treat him royally, not because he is royal by nature. On the contrary, the emperor is a common mortal who has come to stand as head of a nation, by virtue of such not particularly noble processes as birth and breeding.

Yet we behave as if the monarch had noble qualities, and hence blind ourselves to his actual role, which is purely formal and serves to maintain the established order.

William Makepeace Thackeray, *Caricature of Louis XIV*

Hans Tegner, illustration
for *The Emperor's New
Clothes*. It is noteworthy
that the coat of arms
of the emperor's family
is blank; there is no
genealogy

According to the fairy-tale, the emperor was not interested in politics, the army, the arts, or entertainment, but only in clothes. That proves that he was a good emperor. He realized that his power was based on external display, not on inner qualities.

To find out if his subjects also knew this, he put them to the test every time he showed himself in public. Only those able to keep up appearances are suited to their role in society. The Fool, by contrast, has no understanding of the benefits of propriety and shows himself for what he is in his response to the monarch.

This fairy-tale is sometimes mistakenly held up as illustrating the superiority of the innocent child over the pretensions of the adult world. Only children, fools and drunkards are impertinent enough to proclaim the 'truth', much like the enlightened fools among the republican critics of the monarchist system, who are determined to stick to the naked truth, ignoring the mechanism of power politics to which even they owe their position.

Republicanism constitutes a danger to democracy because it does not allow for a king. Without a monarch, democracy collapses.

(Here one might have added a treatise on the role of modern art in testing the ability to see what does not exist, or at least the ability to pretend that something can be seen – the two forces that hold the civilized world

together, namely Fantasy and her sister Propriety. Culture is the product
of a series of more or less successful attempts to keep up appearances.
Where the public no longer has enough energy to pretend that it is
impressed by the works of art put on display, democracy, too, is in danger.)

Not even Till Eulenspiegel claimed that power rests on nothing. He
left the decision to the public. His white sheet was a warning: watch
your tongue; if you say too much, public order collapses. By his ruse,
Till put the court to the test. He probed the citizens' power of imagination, their ability to see something where there was nothing to see,
or the decency to admit their own ignorance. The state is held together
by citizens who act as if the established order had sound foundations,
when, in fact, it is based on a lie. Only the dumb lack the decency to
act dumb.

THE HYPOTHETICAL FOOL

The weavers describe their invisible clothes in detail, specifying all
the colours by name and describing the patterns. The minister in
charge passes the information on to the emperor. It is not long
before everyone, without ever seeing the clothes, is speaking of the
glorious colours and the quality of the material: 'The whole suit is as
light as a cobweb; one might fancy one has nothing at all on, when
dressed in it; that, however, is the great virtue of this delicate cloth.'

In fact the clothes exist only in language. Talk weaves the finest of
textiles. Not the facts but the words are what matters. Rumour constitutes the invisible cloth that binds the established order.

If the emperor's clothes are praised long enough, everyone will
eventually believe in them. In that light, the making of a monarch
follows the logic of the self-fulfilling prophecy.

Yet Hans Christian Andersen's tale is subtler than that. The
emperor's subjects reason as follows: we are not mad, we know perfectly well that the emperor is stark naked. But there are bound to be
fools who believe that monarchs are royal by nature. And to keep from
becoming victims of our rulers and the credulous mob, it is nevertheless worth our while to praise the emperor's clothes.

Here we have the whole problem of man's stupidity in a nutshell.
The fool is always the 'Other'. We secretly despise the hypothetical

Félicien Rops, *The Triumph of the Naked Emperor*

dunce, who is stupid enough to believe in the emperor's clothes. Yet this non-existent dunce determines our actions. To be on the safe side we extol the emperor's invisible clothes, ensuring that all of us become the fools we are so afraid of being.

That is the paradox of the non-existent dunce, who nevertheless makes his presence felt. The real fool, however, is not the hypothetical dunce who does not exist, nor yet the anxious fellow traveller who can be sure of his place in the established order – the real fool is the enlightened citizen who refuses to believe the story of the invisible clothes, who is determined to cling to the naked truth, who refuses to believe in the power of a non-existent dunce. And it is this enlightened fool who joins the ranks of the republican critics of the monarchy and ulti-mately gets the axe.

The monarch's demise, too, starts with a rumour. The bystander does not say, 'I see that the emperor is naked,' but, 'That child says he has nothing on.' There is a close link between rumour and the power of 'the Other'. The Countess of Hesse in the Eulenspiegel story, too, did not say that she could see nothing, but that the other could see nothing: 'It pleases me much as it pleases My Lord, but it does not please the foolish woman in our midst, who says she can see no painting, and my maidens say likewise.' And she added that she was afraid the whole thing was a knavish trick.

Language gives rise to illusion and also puts an end to it: not the empirical truth but rumour tears the fabric apart.

WHO DID NOT KNOW?

The joke is that everyone, the emperor included, knows that he is stark naked. The hapless child who says in public that the emperor has no clothes on, reveals a fact apparent to all. But how is it that the revelation of something so evident should have such disastrous consequences? It spelled not only the end of the emperor but of his empire as well. If everyone knew, who did not know?

The classic answer is that the state, embodied by the monarch, did not know. The monarch, as monarch, must remain deaf, blind and dumb; the monarch as a private person may, however, think what he likes. Anyone who confuses the two is certifiable.

The monarch must keep up appearances, which is why he blithely

Title-page of Adriaan Poirter's *Het masker van de wereld afgetrocken* (The mask of the world torn away, 1646). Medusa hides behind the mask of Mistress World. The hidden truth is likely to turn us to stone

continues to walk on stark naked. And the citizens, as his loyal subjects, must play along with him. As long as everyone acts as if the monarch were dressed, the State is preserved. (The opposite is the case with the character Klinger in the television series M*A*S*H – as long as everyone refuses to see the frocks he wears, for the specific purpose of being thrown out of the army, discipline is maintained.)

STUPIDITY IN THREE PERIODS

Homo pomo est
Man is a fruit
P. C. Hooft

Thanks to Peter Sloterdijk and particularly to Slavoj Žižek (*For They Know Not What They Do*, London, 1991), a morosopher to whose contorted writings I owe a great debt, I am able to specify three periods in the development of stupidity.

To begin with there is *classical stupidity*, characterized by fundamental naivety. Here the biblical: 'Father, forgive them; for they know not what they do,' is readily applied. The fool's picture of reality does not fit the facts. He walks with his head in the clouds and is blind to the world as it is. By tearing away the veil, we can show him the naked truth.

To *modern stupidity*, by contrast, this maxim applies: 'Father, they know not what they do, and it's a good thing . . . '. The veil does not hide the real state of affairs; far from it, reality exists by virtue of illusions. Appearances shape our reality, as long, that is, as the illusion goes unnoticed. Understanding would not only put an end to stupidity and delusion, but also to the world that revolves around them. *Esse est non percipi* – to be is not to be perceived.

This can be illustrated by Raphael's *La Fornarina*. It shows a woman who draws a transparent veil up to her naked breasts. Why the veil? The classical answer is: the veil renders her belly all the more seductive. But on closer examination, the veil is seen to be flesh-coloured, and then the horrible truth begins to dawn. The veil does not hide a seductive belly; the belly is a veil hiding the intestines. (This is reminiscent of the phrase used by Jesuits to suppress sinful thoughts on encountering a beautiful woman or man: a human being is a leather bag filled with shit.) In short, if you know too much, you run the risk of going mad.

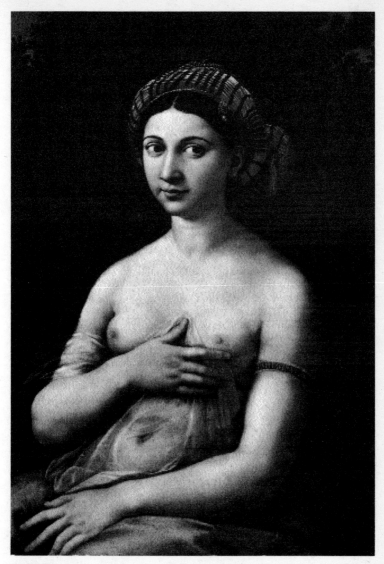

Raphael, *La Fornarina*. (*c.* 1519). Galleria Nazionale d'Arte Antica, Rome.

This form of stupidity, too, has become outdated. Both definitions are rooted in the classical idea that the fool mistakes reality. Nowadays we live under conditions of *post-modern stupidity* ('pomo' in short):

'Father, they do know what they do, but they do it anyway.' Stupidity seems to have gone out of fashion. The postmodernist is much too clever to be fooled by his own rhetoric. He is an enlightened idiot. He is fully aware of the gulf between appearance and essence, but still swears by the mask. We can no longer confront the postmodernist with his blind spot, with what he represses in order to be in the right, because the pomo has already made allowances for that.

Take politics. The politician openly deceives the masses; no one believes him, and he knows that, and we know that he knows, and he knows that as well. Where are we to find stupidity in all this omniscience? When everybody knows, who does not know?

It looks as if we have entered the post-ideological age, but that conclusion would be premature. The pomo leaves the fundamental level of stupidity intact: stupidity is at work in reality itself, in what we do, not in what we think we are doing.

We know very well that the monarch's power is based on certain trade-offs, but in practice we behave as if the king were the embodiment of the people. We are fools in practice. Stupidity does not lie in thinking, (we know better than that); stupidity lies in doing it anyway.

In short, we must stop looking for stupidity on the psychological plane; stupidity has nothing personal or spontaneous about it, quite the contrary. Stupidity is materialized in everyday practice. Stupidity lurks in action, to the extent that stupidity can be delegated to machines.

THE FAME MACHINE (WITH NO STATE GUARANTEE)

To understand the workings of a machine that helps to preserve our constitutional monarchy, we should study the fame machine described in Villiers de l'Isle Adam's *La machine à gloire* (1883).

We are told that the engineer Baron Bathybius Bottom, 'the apostle of Utility', invented a machine that could manufacture fame by organic means. But is it really possible to produce Fame (an intellectual end) with a machine (a physical means)? To solve that problem, Bottom looked to the claque, a group of people hired to applaud a play and turn it into a success.

All fame has its claque, that is, its shadow side, its part in deception, in mechanical tricks and in Nothing (for Nothing is the
origin of all things).

In principle, just one man laughing in public is enough to set off an
entire audience.

And since we are loath to have laughed for nothing, or to be
carried away by the laughter of others, we allow that the play is
amusing.

The claque is a living monument to the inability of the masses to judge
the value of what they hear: 'The claque is to theatrical Fame what the
Wailing Women used to be to the Bereaved.' In so-called primitive
societies, women were hired to cry at funerals on behalf of the next of
kin. The heirs did their duty through others while attending to more
pressing business – the division of the estate. Here, mention should
also be made of the role of the chorus in Greek tragedy. The spectators
came to the theatre weighed down with their own problems and
unable to summon up compassion for the characters on stage. The
chorus therefore felt compassion in their stead.

Bottom set himself the task of replacing the claque with a more
reliable instrument. The problem was to get the audience to feel the
emotions by which the Spirit of the Majority would adopt the machine's
crude expressions of fame.

The machine Bottom invented is in fact the auditorium itself. Every
play performed in it is hailed as a masterpiece by the gilded putti and
caryatids, from whose mouths pour laughter, sobs and calls for encores.
In addition, pipes filled with laughing gas and tear gas have been
installed, balconies with metal fists to shake the audience awake, and
catapults for flinging bouquets.

And then occurs the fascinating phenomenon that justifies the use
of the applause machine. Individuals prefer not to flout public opinion.
Everyone is convinced of the truth of the axiom: 'That man is a success,
so, despite the fools and the envious, he must be a famous and capable
person. To play safe, we had better take his side, if only not to look like
imbeciles.' This is the covert argument pervading the atmosphere of
the auditorium.

No matter how unmoved the spectator may be, he is easily carried away by the general enthusiasm, by what is happening all around him. Such is the *force des choses*. Soon he, too, will applaud thunderously and uncritically. He is, as ever, completely at one with the Majority. And if only he could, he would make more noise than the Machine itself, for fear of drawing attention to himself.

Fame now makes its actual entry in the auditorium, and the illusory aspect of the Bottom Apparatus disappears by dissolving in the radiance of the Truth. The use of the machine in parliament is currently under consideration . . .

MODERN RITUAL

On the Queen's Birthday there is general rejoicing, which is shared by nobody.
Simon Carmiggelt

What is majesty? According to the critics majesty is nothing but show. According to monarchists, majesty is found whenever the mere mention of the royal house gives rise to feelings of reverence. According to me, majesty is enshrined in symbols apparent to all: national anthems, flags, commemorative tiles. The more varied the expressions to which the monarch gives rise, the greater is his majesty, the greater the respect he inspires.

To cheer on the constitutional monarchy, nowadays we have a perfected version of the fame machine. The stupidity inherent in ceremonial rites has been delegated to television. Television is stupid on our behalf; it performs the duties by which society is held together.

Thus a single Dutch town is selected each year to pay homage to the queen on behalf of the rest of the nation. Her ceremonial visit to that town is shown live on television. But in principle the same tape could be replayed each year. In the knowledge that the television is transmitting the nation's ritual homage to the queen, we can switch off with an easy conscience. Television is not susceptible to argument. In this way the future of the constitutional monarchy is guaranteed.

Don't get me wrong: I am not attacking the monarchy or democracy, and certainly not the combination of both kinds of stupidity enshrined in a constitutional monarchy. Nor am I holding a brief for irrationality. I simply note the need for ritual follies in which is embedded the idiocy that necessarily lies at the heart of our existence. We must never forget the fictional character of the world. Real stupidity reigns where everyone thinks that everything is self-evident.

A FINAL NOTE: CANNED LAUGHTER

In the tradition of Villiers, Slavoj Žižek explains the function of canned laughter on television. What is this laughter for? First of all, it tells us when we ourselves are expected to laugh. Laughter is a duty. *Ride si sapis* – laugh if thou art wise. By your laughter you show your neighbours that you understand the joke, that you are worthy of their company. Laughter creates a bond between know-alls. We pretend that what we are watching is funny, and this sham holds society together.

Gummbah, *Time Passes Slowly* (1998)

Nor is that all, for most of the time we do not laugh. But that is no disaster – canned laughter absolves us even from the duty to laugh. It laughs for us. Hence even if our heart is not in it, and we are staring stupidly at the screen, after the event we can nevertheless say that, thanks to the canned laughter we have been thoroughly entertained. Meanwhile we can think about something completely different, allow our minds to wander, undertake a philosophical excursion, empathize with the actors – whatever.

Axel, another of Villiers de l'Isle-Adam's heroes, had as a motto: 'Living is something our servants do for us.' In line with that dictum, we can say: laughing, crying, showing compassion, is what our machines do for us. Machines perform the stupid rituals that keep our world together.

Incidentally, research was undertaken several years ago into the behaviour of viewers during comedy series using taped laughter. It turned out that the viewers thought afterwards that they had laughed their heads off, while videotapes of the audience proved the opposite.

We take the world shown on television with a pinch of salt. As enlightened fools we sit back and relax. Being stupid is something the world does for us, thus enabling us to look wise to the world. Keeping our ironical distance, we view the foolish spectacle.

All the same, this huge joke shapes our actions and our thinking, including the idea that the world is stupid and we ourselves enlightened viewers.

EIGHT

The Darwin Awards

1 Ecstasy

NOMINATIONS

The Darwin Awards are bestowed each year via the Internet on those who have made an invaluable contribution to evolution by – unintentionally - removing their weak genes from the reproductive process. Because the winners are always dead, the prize has never been handed over. Recently, those who as a consequence of their stupidity have been sterilized, castrated, or otherwise reproductively challenged, have also been made eligible for the Award.

Candidates can be submitted for the following categories: games and entertainment, work and industry, weapons and explosives, love, suicide, hunting, crime and punishment, traffic, religion, and medical treatment. Laureates have included the following:

> The 64-year-old throat-cancer patient, Abraham Mosley, who tried to light a cigar in a Florida hospital and managed to set fire to both the bandage round his neck and to his pyjamas. Because his vocal cords had been removed, he could not call for help and was burned alive in his bed.

> The bungee-jumper who had gauged the length of his rope against the depth of the gorge, but forgot the rope was elastic.

> The leader of a Christian sect in Los Angeles, who made a daily attempt to follow in Christ's footsteps and walk on water. He died unexpectedly on 24 November 1999 when he slipped on a bar of soap while practising in his bathtub.

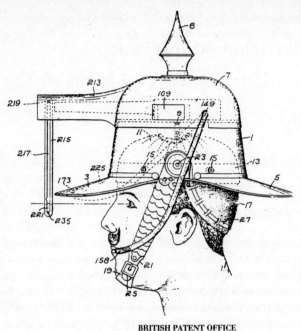

BRITISH PATENT OFFICE
Convention Date (United States), July 14, 1915.
Application Date (United Kingdom), July 11, 1916.
No. 9759 16.

Albert B. Pratt's shooting helmet, patented in New York in 1915

Three Palestinian terrorists who set off for Israel with explosives having set their watches for wintertime, which begins earlier in Israel than elsewhere because of morning prayers. The timebombs, however, were set for summertime, because Palestinians in the occupied territories refuse to live by what they call Zionist time. As a result the bombs went off earlier than intended, and the terrorists blew themselves up.

Albert B. Pratt of Lyndon (USA), who invented a shooting helmet with a built-in revolver, is a perennial favourite. By tugging on a cord with his teeth, the wearer can fire a bullet. It is a mystery how the patent for this device was ever granted, seeing that the guinea-pig's neck must have been broken by the recoil on firing the first shot. The helmet is a patent aid to suicide.

Congratulations to all the winners! These examples illustrate in weird and wonderful ways the stupidity that keeps our civilization rolling.

STUPIDITY AS THE BASIS OF CIVILIZATION

Stupidity is unwitting self-destruction, the ability to act against one's best interests, with death as the extreme result. This talent is typically human. To begin with, man is the only species stupid enough to attract the attention of wild animals by the cries he utters at birth. In addition, man comes into the world a livid purple so that he lacks the protective colouring needed to vanish in the undergrowth. Moreover, man is one of the few mammals unable to walk at birth.

Worse still, while animals have retained an instinct for self-preservation, man is capable of risking his own survival and that of his species on a whim. For the sake of delusions concerning race, nation, sex or religion, we are prepared to sacrifice ourselves and our fellow men.

On the one hand stupidity poses a daily threat to civilization; on the other it constitutes the mystical foundation of our existence. For if man was not to fall victim to his own stupidity, he had to develop his intelligence. All the strategies aimed at controlling our stupidity combine to form our civilization. Culture is a time- and place-conditioned product of a series of more or less abortive attempts to come to grips with the self-destructive folly found in all countries and at all times.

AN EXPLOSIVE MIXTURE

Stupidity forced man to develop his intelligence, but intelligence is no guarantee of self-preservation. Indeed, intelligence can boost stupidity. The explosive character of this blend is revealed most spectacularly during hostilities. Less conspicuously, stupidity comes to the surface in the smouldering civil war we wage on the highways, which, worldwide, causes hundreds of thousands of fatalities every year – not to mention the innumerable serious injuries. (Incidentally, 70 per cent of the contestants in the Paralympics are road accident victims.) This chronic catastrophe makes less of an impression than a one-off spectacular disaster, such as an aeroplane crash.

The explosive mix of stupidity and intelligence can also be found in technological advances:

Low-nicotine tobacco has doubled consumption of cigarettes.

Energy-saving light bulbs are used mainly for the decorative illumination of gardens.

Motorists who have airbags and seatbelts drive on average 20 per cent faster.

More highways create more traffic; more lanes on the roads cause more queues.

Zebra crossings lead to more accidents involving pedestrians.

To prevent the destruction of police cameras by speed demons, cameras have been installed to keep an eye on the speed cameras.

The sturdier the chassis of a car, the harder it is to free the casualties trapped inside.

Air conditioning affects the ozone layer, and contributes to the greenhouse effect. The cooling of offices, in other words, leads to the heating of the atmosphere.

Mad cows are the result of recycled butchers' waste.

The consumption of paper in offices has increased since the introduction of computers.

The development of cushioned jogging shoes intended to protect the knees has increased wear and tear on the hips.

With the development of software for solving complicated problems more quickly, minor faults now lead to more serious consequences.

Filters for purifying tap water have proved an ideal breeding ground for bacteria.

Better hygiene has led to greater susceptibility to germs. The successful suppression of bacterial infections has contributed to the spread of new viral infections such as AIDS/HIV.

Suntan lotion is now said to cause skin cancer.

Elsewhere, too, intelligent stupidity can be caught red-handed:

The restoration of the Michelangelo frescoes in the Sistine Chapel attracted so many visitors that the higher humidity, the increased temperature and the sulphur concentration in the air led to invisible acid rain in the chapel. Cleaning causes pollution.

The No. 5 tram, the so-called Amsterdam 'Speed Line', regularly drives straight past crowded tram stops. When passengers complained, the Public Transport Office explained that trams would not be able to keep to the timetable if they picked up passengers at every tram stop.

Life-threatening stupidity cannot be eradicated without eradicating mankind, which would be tantamount to stupidity squared. The only solution is to devise lasting new stratagems for dealing with stupidity. Seen in such a light, stupidity is the engine that drives our civilization.

CUNNING STUPIDITY

One of the most daring ploys for coming to grips with stupidity is to promote self-sacrifice as the highest expression of neighbourly love. It is not for nothing that martyrdom plays an important role in most religions: the triumph of stupidity.

Consider the great hunger artists of the past. In times of scarcity the proud man makes a virtue out of necessity. Starvation is presented as a form of ascesis, as an ethical ideal. Nowadays, we are familiar with fasting as an *aesthetic* ideal, as witness the anorexics who strut down the catwalk as models of beauty – stupidity *à la mode*.

Johnny Hart, 'We've tried every possible way', cartoon from *Hey! B.C.* ([1958] London, 1971)

By making falsifiability a criterion of scientific truth, we turn self-destruction into a step towards progress. A scientist is expected to specify by what experiments his theory can be refuted.

We set up idealistic institutions whose ultimate aim is their own dissolution.

According to Erasmus, stupidity turns into bliss when man loses himself in God. This mystical experience is indistinguishable from temporary madness. The ecstatic mystic is beyond himself, just like the madman. In rapture his soul leaves his body momentarily to fuse with the Highest Object of his desire. Man's passionate longing for God resembles the love between man and woman: it is an erotic experience in which the lovers lose themselves to find themselves anew in the other. In spiritual ecstasy, the Christian lover is given a foretaste of eternal bliss. Erasmus calls it erotic madness.

According to Erasmus, divine ecstasy is not reserved for mystics but is experienced by everyone who forgets himself when reading a book. The life of a chosen exegete, seized by the spirit, is characterized by astonishment, spiritual intoxication and rapture. 'If you approach them humbly, with piety and veneration, you will feel yourself ineffably breathed upon by the Godhead, seized, caught up, transfigured; you will see the wealth of that richest Solomon, the hidden treasure of eternal Wisdom'. (The translation can be found in Erasmus, *Ecstasy and the Praise of Folly*, translated by M. A. Screech, London, 1988, p. 239)

THE LAPSE

All myths about the origin of the human race suggest the existence of some intermediary stage in which man was no longer an animal but not yet human.

Materialist theories postulate a sudden aberration, a lapse of nature, a monstrous deviation that forced the human animal to develop his logos, or reason, in order to limit the damage.

According to the idealist school, all our troubles started with the introduction of logos, as witness the theft of fire by Prometheus, and Adams's Fall. In the first case, the human animal was handed the magic spark that the Gnostics sometimes referred to as 'pneuma'; in the second case man himself took the initiative by eating of the forbidden fruit. In both cases there was a breach of a (mythical) law of nature. Animal egotism, whose purpose is self-preservation, was changed into self-destructive egoism, which subjects nature to its bizarre laws.

With the acquisition of logos, things ceased to be self-evident. Contrary to the commonplace that, bound by his finite, mortal, all-too-human nature, man can never become wholly reasonable, reason seems to prevent man from becoming human. Unlike animals, which follow their instincts blindly, man is structurally alienated from himself.

Logos is a parasite that disrupts the vital rhythm of the human animal, and subjects it to an autonomous law. It replaces spontaneous feelings and insights with ready-made patterns, opposed to our natural needs, with stress as the consequence. Humanization is mutilation: witness the compulsive neurosis of raccoons, parrots, fish and other domesticated animals. A prime example is the well-trained horse heroically carrying its master until it drops dead. The proud steed has lost its animality and bears witness to self-destructive stupidity in its most glorious form.

Man is branded by stupidity. But is logos the cause of his stupidity or did it emerge as a reaction to stupidity?

(For stylistic reasons, I use such words as logos, reason, understanding, intellect and intelligence as synonyms, unless I state otherwise. Using Aristotle's definition of man as *animal rationale*, I consider these terms so many tokens of the cognitive power distinguishing man from animal. '*Sapienti sat.*')

FORBIDDEN FRUIT

It is an illusion to think that stupidity precedes intelligence or vice versa, as if there were a boundary separating stupidity from logos. Stupidity and reason cannot do without each other. Take the Fall of Man. By eating of the tree of the knowledge of good and evil, Adam acquired the kind of insight that enabled him to look back on his deed and see that it was stupid and evil. With this lapse, man became an animal conscious of his mistakes: witness the birth of laughter.

BURIDAN'S ASS

Stultus semper incipit vivere
A fool is always at the beginning of his life.

In front of me is a bag of apples, from which I am allowed to pick just one. Freedom is the ability to choose, after considering the pros and cons, without external compulsion. However, at a given point I must cut the knot or else I will fare like Buridan's ass, which starved to death because it could not choose between two identical haystacks.

Every development starts with a blind choice, a precipitous decision that cannot be reduced to a demonstrable cause. The principle of insufficient reason – I did it because I did it, not for any particular cause – breaks the chain of causality.

However, the blind choice of just one aspect among many in an undifferentiated whole creates new order out of chaos.

To put it more dramatically: stupidity is at work in every decision. Every time we make up our minds, we open up the abyss of idiocy. Every choice, however trivial, is a leap into the dark.

THE CASTLE IN THE AIR

It was once said that to move a planet, you need but find the
point of leverage: therefore, I, seeking to overturn a mind
that was perfect, had to find a point of leverage, and that point
was stupidity.

Stanislav Lem, *Cyberiad*

We must try to grasp logos by its irrational roots, before it assumes
the features of logos. Every logical concept by which we try to come
to grips with reality is structurally stupid. Every attempt to put sense
into nonsense is madness. The imposition of order is irrevocably a
disruption of order. Stupidity clings to logos like some latent original
sin that keeps compelling man to prove himself. As soon as man starts
to think, the firm ground slips from under his feet, forcing him some-
how to build his castles in the air.

There you have the crux of the matter: our thinking is rooted in
stupidity, in the irrational core that is the *sine qua non* of possibility
and impossibility, the source of our energy and a permanent threat
to our existence. Without stupidity, logos would collapse. Stupidity
enables us to attain a modicum of identity, however mangled.
Stupidity, in short, has a positive function. But as soon as it gains the
upper hand, stupidity changes from a salutary impulse into an all-
destructive force.

This puts us in possession of the parts of a paradox machine,
something we have seen turning its wheels throughout the pages of
this Schoolmen's *pons asinorum*. Another instance is the installation
by the artist Jean Tinguely, built in order to destroy itself in 'Homage
to New York'. By deliberately cutting its life short, the work of art was
intended to undermine the standards defining a work of art. The
demonstration took place on 17 March 1960 in the Sculpture Garden
of the Museum of Modern Art in New York, and proved a successful
failure, since the enormous mechanism consisting of bicycle wheels,
chains and a dismantled piano broke down prematurely . . .

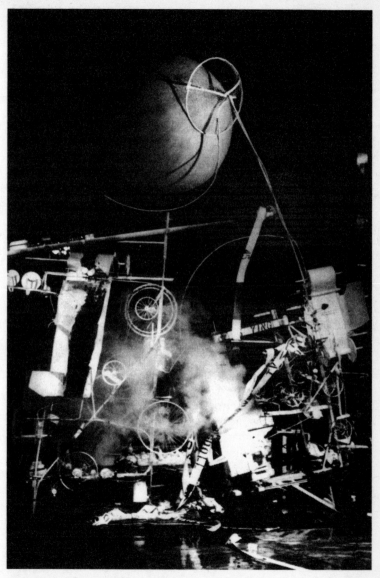

Jean Tinguely, *Homage to New York*, a self-destructive work of art, demonstrated in the sculpture garden of the Museum of Modern Art, New York on 17 March 1960

GATEKEEPERS

You cannot step outside the castle of knowledge, in order to establish that it is hanging in the air without going mad. Every attempt to expose the stupidity of wisdom is an abysmal act of folly which puts our thinking at risk. The stupidity of wisdom can only be accessed through the absurdities in the path of thinking: sophisms, jokes, paradoxes.

WHO AM I?

What time is it? If no one asks me, I know the answer, but when I try to explain it to someone who asks, then I no longer know.

St Augustine, *Confessions*

Using a variant of St Augustine's dictum about time, we can say: if nobody asks who I am, I know the answer, but as soon as I try to explain I no longer know. 'I do not comprehend all I am. The mind is too confined to grasp itself. But what is it that man does not comprehend about himself? Might it be something outside, and not inside him? I am filled with surprise, deep surprise; I am perplexed' (*Confessions*). The question of my identity throws up an obstacle thanks to which I no longer know myself, while the knowledge of who I am transforms me. Self-understanding stands in the way of self-knowledge.

THE BOEOTIAN SPHINX

'What goes on four feet, on two feet, and three, but the more feet it goes on the weaker it be?' Anyone unable to answer the riddle of the Sphinx of Thebes was thrown into the abyss. Oedipus gave the answer: man as a child, as an adult and as an old man. The power of the Sphinx over mankind was broken, and she hurled herself into the depths.

This story is often read as an example of liberation from superstition. Once man has discovered himself, mythology plunges into the abyss.

'Sapientia edificavit sibi domum'; title-page woodcut from *De ascensu et descensu intellectus* (Valencia, 1512), a treatise written in 1304 by the Catalan mystic Ramón Lull. It introduces three intellectual 'stairways'. By the side of the two concentric circles in the wheel on the left, a staircase with eight steps, a *scala intellectualis*, on which the categories of the Great Chain of Being are set out in hierarchic order. Each step names the subjects and objects illustrated on the right. The steps are (from the bottom): stone, flame, plant and animal, with the lion as an example. These lower steps comprise palpable nature. Then comes man, who inhabits nature, but none the less reaches into the higher stages thanks to his God-given reason. The next step is Heaven, with space for the angels and for God. The last step leads to the castle of knowledge, the *summum bonum*.

Lull comments: 'We set out from imperfection, so that we may mount to perfection, but conversely we can fall from perfection to imperfection. On the banner of the neophyte at the bottom of the staircase, we read *Intellectus conjunctus*, which alludes to the 'integral understanding' the neophyte seeks. The banner at the top of the print tells us that wisdom has built her own house.

But was Oedipus' answer correct? What of the disasters that followed? Thebes was stricken by pestilence; the House of Cadmus perished; Oedipus murdered his father; Jocasta committed suicide when she discovered that she had married her son; their sons murdered one another and their daughter Antigone was walled up alive in a tomb where she hanged herself. According to some, the Sphinx was not asking about man himself but about his being.

The solution of the fatal riddle is a trick, a joke, a turn of phrase thanks to which the question becomes its own answer: man is someone who is at a loss when faced with monsters and the riddles they pose to him.

According to the *Tabula Cebetis*, the Sphinx is stupidity personified.

MAN'S BEING

Become who you are!
Pindar

Stupidity stops man from becoming reasonable while being the basis of his identity. Utter amazement at his stupidity defines man as *Homo sapiens*. Man is shaped by shame, fury and remorse at his failures, which constantly spur him to prove himself. Man becomes man in vain efforts to live up to his own image. Viewed in that light, man himself is the missing link between animal and man. We are therefore part of a vicious circle: man becomes man in the struggle with stupidity that prevents him from becoming man.

In short, thought is ecstatic in character: our mind is formed as a reaction to the folly characteristic of man and at the same time alien to him. Man is by definition beside himself.

The man who is truly himself, on the other hand, is not of this world. Whosoever finds himself is hopelessly lost, like the racing cyclist who collapses as soon as he hits his own limits. Apart from a near-death experience, there is nothing as baffling as a near-I experience.

Title-page woodcut for Charles de Bovelles, *Liber de intellectu* (Paris, 1510). On the left, we see Fortuna (Chance), blindfolded, seated on a ball teetering above a pit. She holds the wheel of fortune that bears a king, a falling prince, a slave and someone about to take the prince's place. On the right Sapientia (Wisdom), holding a mirror, is ensconced on a solid throne. According to Bovelles, man is estranged from himself by his stupidity. He has ceased to be himself. Once he was the image of God, but he has fallen off his throne and has been bestialized. 'Man has become the very opposite of man.' The fool lives from day to day, and wastes his time. Wisdom alone, knowledge of one's proper place in the cosmic order, endows man's life with balance and direction. Self-understanding leads to *philautia*, self-love: 'only he who knows himself human, is a man, is at one with himself.'

ERRARE HUMANUM EST

There's an imbecile inside me. I must profit from his mistakes.
Paul Valéry, *Cahiers* (1910)

The cliché that to err is human apparently reflects tolerance of human weakness, but in fact defines man: man does not differ from animals by his superior wisdom, but by his stupidity, by his ability to lapse into self-made illusions. Unlike the ass, man bumps into one and the same stone time and again. He learns nothing from history but is condemned to repeat the same mistakes endlessly.

On the other hand, man has turned his errors and the shame that goes with them into so many props of church and public morality. Science has embraced error as a road to truth. To put it even more strongly, we have learned to enjoy our blunders as if they were choice moments. We take pleasure in displeasure, as witness comedy and tragedy.

BLOOMERS

One of the most popular BBC television programmes is 'Auntie's Bloomers', in which viewers are shown extracts from television series and news broadcasts that had to be discarded because a piece of scenery collapsed, a journalist fluffed his lines, or an actor stumbled on a doorstep.

The programme apparently owes its fame to the breaking of a taboo: it exposes the hidden role played by failures in success. However, the bloomers have lost their subversive power. We know that every triumph is built of ups and downs. The revelation actually contributes to our admiration of the result. That is why Tommy Cooper could give away the secret of his conjuring trick without destroying its magic effect. In fact, the blunders themselves became the main attraction.

What the bloomers hide from us is the share of the eerie mechanism that decides what is successful and what is not. To gain some idea of the intangible force that pulls the strings behind the screen, we need only think of the tyrannical viewing statistics which determine what we are shown on television, even though no one knows the guinea pigs who view and judge television programmes on our behalf.

Still more blatant is the stupid intervention of the laughter machine, which laughs joylessly to maintain the illusion that what is being shown is highly comical even if the viewer is bored to tears.

Even during bloomer programmes a laughter machine is used, because the producer is no longer sure of the programme's laughter-evoking effect. This can lead to some strange breakdowns in communication. One of the most remarkable blunders involved a laughter machine that went off at the wrong moment during a comedy programme. This bloomer was nevertheless accompanied by the antics of a laughter machine that laughed on our behalf.

Bloomers from comedy series constitute a special category. Strictly speaking, our laughter is directed at jokes that have fluffed. It is all too reminiscent of a child ordering its father to laugh for no good reason, whereupon the father bursts out laughing at the stupidity of the request.

Here a latent order comes to the surface: we do not laugh because the jokes are funny – the jokes appear funny because we laugh at them. The rules and laws that govern our lives owe their authority not to their reasonable character but to our sheep-like docility.

The perverse character of this order is revealed in such stupid – because self-defeating – commands as: Be impulsive! Don't think! Stop obeying!

The master of toying with hidden conventions was Tommy Cooper. When the audience laughed feebly at one of his weak jokes, he gestured to them to laugh more loudly while looking anxiously into the wings as if the stage director were catching up on him. The audience laughed in response to this exhortation to laugh. The conspiracy helped to fool the man behind the curtain – who represented authority. The comic owed his success to the laughter, not to the quality of his jokes. Laughter is a social duty, with jokes as an alibi.

When Tommy Cooper died on stage, the audience died laughing.

SECOND NATURE

Habit frees us from the necessity of having to think about everything. Without a fixed frame of reference we should have to constantly reconsider the fluctuating situations in which we find ourselves. The rituals of propriety, which regulate our social relations, relieve us of worries about mutual tensions and allow us to concentrate on the conversation. And we can only speak spontaneously by blindly observing the grammatical rules. Rhetoric abounds in platitudes for channelling our thoughts, which can only develop if the rules of logic have become second nature.

As soon as we become aware of automatisms, our thoughts cease to range freely. The pianist stumbles over the keys if he thinks about the fingering. The walker loses his balance if he pays attention to the rhythm of his steps. Dumb habit is no obstacle to free development. Enlightened thought does not prove its worth in the fight against routine; rules have a liberating effect as long as we follow them unthinkingly.

Our intellectual creativity can only flourish within conceptual limitations. The spirit thrives by grace of the dead letter, on condition that we ignore this fact. Stupidity, in short, is a prerequisite for intellectual growth.

HYPOTHETICAL STUPIDITY AND TOILET PAPER

Stupidity does not even have to exist in order to be effective. Before the fall of the Berlin Wall, there was often a shortage of toilet paper in the Eastern Bloc. Yet at one point, and to everyone's amazement, a surfeit of toilet paper appeared in the shops. Soon afterwards the rumour spread that the paper was about to run out, whereupon everybody rushed to the shops and the paper was quickly sold out.

This is a classic example of a self-fulfilling prophecy, taken from *The Yawning Heights*, a novel by the Russian logician Alexander Zinoviev.

Would reliable information have helped to prevent the panic reaction of buyers? No, because the good citizen argues as follows: 'I know perfectly well that there is a surplus of toilet paper, but there are bound to be idiots who believe the rumours, so it is well worth laying in a supply of paper for myself.'

So, even if stupidity does not exist, it still produces an effect. Consider too the notorious, invisible hand of the market. (Cf. Rasto Mocnik, *Über die Bedeutung der Chimären für die conditio humana* [On the bearing of chimeras on the human condition], Vienna, 1986) Without stupidity and illusion the world would collapse.

THE CRUX OF THE MATTER

Whether it be an economy, a kingdom or a character, every structure – however universal – hinges on some form of idiocy, however peculiar. This idiocy can assume the shape of an apple on which a spoilt child has set his mind. Purple with rage, he hangs upside down in his chair, mewling and whimpering for the forbidden fruit as if his life depends on it. Here we are witness to the original sin that may mark the child's mind for the rest of its life.

Take the philatelist who lost his collection when he went bankrupt after spending a fortune on a single rare stamp. Or the president who risked his position by exploring his assistant's vagina with a cigar. Or Iman Wilkins, who believes that studies of climate, fauna, flora, culture and topography prove that Homer's *Iliad* and *Odyssey* were set partly in The Netherlands. Delft is Delphi, Drente is Thrace, Zierikzee is inhabited by the enchantress Circe. He places the entrance to the underworld in Zeeland. Wilkens has built an encyclopædic system of knowledge around this fantasm, one of which many a classical scholar could be proud.

Elsewhere, places of pilgrimage have been founded around the site of a meteorite. At thirteen sites, Jesus' foreskin is worshipped (three were mentioned by Calvin, among them Charroux Abbey near Poitiers, the Church of St John Lateran in Rome and Hildesheim Abbey in Saxony). Moreover, the legitimacy of kingdoms can often be vested in relics that are more insignificant than the pea under the seven times seven mattresses on which the fairy-tale princess slept.

An obsession with idiocy can make or break a man.

THE STONE OF CONTENTION

The Devil put God's omnipotence to the test by asking Him to make a stone so heavy that He could not lift it. What was God to do? If He could not lift the rock, then He was not omnipotent; if He could lift it, then He was not capable of making it heavy enough.

Does God in his perfection stand above the laws of his creation or is he himself subject to them? This paradox proved to be more than a Scholastic game, it touched the very heart of metaphysics. The problem drove Basilides in the second century to the heretical view that the cosmos was the frivolous and malicious improvization of deranged demiurges.

In the eleventh century the issue led to the rise of the antidialectical movement, which placed the concept of God outside the boundaries of reason; in imitation of Tertullian, theologians repeated the paradox *credo quia absurdum est*. In his perfection, God can do the impossible.

Christianity tried to escape from the dilemma of perfection by introducing the idea of infinity: Isaiah's dream of the vegetarian lion would only be realized at the end of time.

According to an English Renaissance commentary, God still keeps trying vainly to prove his omnipotence, with the expanding universe as a consequence.

PARADISE DAMNED

Stupidity looms up like a brick wall. Stupidity undoes all man's attempts to transcend himself. But just imagine a world without stupidity. Our most brilliant inspirations would be realized without effort; everyone would be capable of grasping the deeper meaning of our existence; the reasonable would be self-evident and uncontested. With stupidity, human liberty and freedom of choice would be abolished. Things would lose their name and their significance, because they would all have become equally valuable or worthless. We would live like angels under an eternally radiant sky, yearning for some uprising; like creatures in a suffocating paradise, pining for the Fall.

3 HOLY MADNESS

NASREDDIN

> Nasreddin, Leader of the Dervishes, Master of the hidden treasure, a perfect man. Many say, 'I wanted to learn but have found nothing here but madness.' Yet if they sought deep wisdom elsewhere, they might well have failed to discover it.
>
> Ablahi Mutlaq, 'The Perfect Idiot', *The Doctrines of Nasreddin* (1617)

Khoja Nasreddin (*c.* 1208–85), the holy fool from Anatolia, is part of a long chain of morosophs, wise fools and foolish sages. He is both the sly mocker, and the stupid victim. This explains why so many pranks and acts of stupidity by Nasreddin (and related figures such as Abul-Fath, Juba, Abu Seid and Till Eulenspiegel) have been passed down to us.

Every so often Nasreddin would have right on his side, but still succeed in making himself insufferable with his uncompromising views, thus revealing to us the terrorist potential of idealism.

On other occasions he would follow a delusion, but because his actions were not based on selfish considerations, his obstinacy would gain him respect, thus revealing the holy aspect of stupidity.

Nasreddin illustrates the folly of wisdom as well as the wisdom of folly. At the point where folly and wisdom cross, we impinge on the foundations of our civilization.

Tradition dictates that anyone who broaches the subject of Nasreddin must tell at least seven stories about him (all my examples are taken from Jismath Slobex, *Morosofia universalis*, Salée, 1957).

I: THE ENCYCLOPÆDIA

At the invitation of a group of scholars, Nasreddin went to a teahouse. At the table sat a geographer, a chronicler and an astronomer, all making enthusiastic plans for a universal encyclopædia. 'It has to contain everything.' 'Everything?' asked Nasreddin. 'Everything,' the company assured him.

Nasreddin thought for a moment. 'In that case it will have to contain the entry "encyclopædia", and that entry will have to contain the entire encyclopædia, including the entry "encyclopædia", and so *ad infinitum.*' The scholars looked askance at one another.

'If you look in the book for your own name, then you will have to read all there is about yourself, including this last sentence, "Looks for his own name in the encyclopædia."' The agitation around the table grew.

'Now imagine the geographer looking for his own name in the encyclopædia that he has written himself; since he already knew that his name was in it, he had no need to look it up or to mention it.' The geographer shifted awkwardly in his chair.

'And if I look up my own biography and start to read everything about me from the first blessed moment that I came into the world, then I shall be dead by the time I get to the middle of the entry.' The chronicler at last saw his chance of correcting Nasreddin: 'In that case you cannot have reached the middle.' 'Is that my fault or the encyclopædia?' Nasreddin asked, whereupon the historian shamefacedly took a sip of his tea.

The editors sat around the table dismayed. They resolved unanimously that in future the only book they would consult – apart from the Koran – would be the book of nature.

II: THE BIGGEST FOOL

Sitting back to front on his ass (to make certain that he was going the right way), Khoja Nasreddin rode into the city of Aksehir. When he passed three shepherds seated in the shade of a teahouse, he fetched a gold coin from his threadbare coat and flung it into their midst, calling out that it was for the biggest fool. The three then tried to outdo one another with tales proving their stupidity. The first told how he had smashed a fly on his forehead with a stone. 'That's nothing compared with my stupidity', said the second, 'I sowed salt in my field.' 'That's nothing compared with my stupidity', said the third, 'I was unable to find the ass on which I myself was sitting.' They continued to boast about their folly until sunset. When at last they realized that their attempts to outwit each other stood in the way of the successful demonstration of their stupidity, they returned the gold coin to Nasreddin, who thanked them for an enjoyable afternoon. Under a star-studded sky, he continued his profitable travels.

No man is intelligent enough to grasp his own stupidity. The moment we start thinking, we are trapped in a vicious circle of concepts that refer back to themselves. There is no final guarantee of the logical soundness of thought. Our intellect tries to no avail to get a grip on itself, just like a snake trying to swallow its own tail. In this way, logos thwart its own success – a case of self-destructive stupidity.

Yet stupidity is also the driving force of thought, since our wisdom grows in its vain attempts to come to grips with itself.

III: HAPPINESS FAVOURS THE FOOLISH

Nasreddin was lying in the grass staring at the sky when a disciple approached him and asked, 'What is happiness?' Nasreddin thought for a long time, then boxed the disciple's ears before kissing him on each cheek. Perplexed, the disciple asked for an explanation. 'Your question put an end to my happiness. But then I found happiness in puzzling over your question.'

As soon as the sage wonders what it means to live a happy life, he raises a problem that, according to Aristotle, stands in the way of happiness. Nothing is any longer what it seems. Yet the philosopher finds happiness in contemplating happiness.

IV: THE EIGHTEENTH CAMEL

A father left instructions that, after his death, half his fortune was to go to his oldest son, a third to his second son, and a ninth to his youngest. Alas, his fortune consisted of seventeen camels. In vain did the sons look for a way of solving the problem without having to cut the camels into pieces. Just then Nasreddin rode past. He suggested adding his own camel to the rest, so that there was a total of eighteen camels. 'The oldest gets half, which makes nine camels. The second son gets a third, which makes six. The youngest gets one ninth, which makes two camels. They all add up to seventeen camels. One is left over, and that one is mine.' Whereupon Nasreddin rode on.

In 1911 the German philosopher Hans Vaihinger published *The Philosophy of As-If*, in which he mentions hundreds of examples of unproven or improvable hypotheses that nevertheless had tangible effects on the personal, social and scientific spheres, whereupon they became superfluous. The ego, the soul, freedom and responsibility, but also manners, botanical systems and the figure zero are useful fictions, no less so than the eighteenth camel. However, we only arrive at the desired result when we discard the temporary expedients as having fulfilled their purpose.

Only the believer confuses fiction with established fact. He does not use his fabrications to fathom the world, but uses the world to confirm his delusions. Thus even a silly misunderstanding can become the centre of a worldwide cult.

V: THE HOLY ASS

When Nasreddin had finished his discipleship, his master presented him with an ass. Nasreddin left the mosque, which was built around the tomb of a saint, and made for the Anatolian highlands. On the way he was given so few alms that he thought it best to teach his ass to eat less and less. Every day he halved his ration of oats, until the ass got no more than a handful in twenty-four hours. That same night, the ass died of starvation. Nasreddin was beside himself with grief. He buried the ass and mourned for days beside the grave. Passers-by asked why he was so sad, whereupon Nasreddin pointed to the burial mound and said: 'My best friend.' Deeply moved by his sorrow they became convinced that his friend must have been a saint. Their gifts grew and not long afterwards Nasreddin had enough money to build a magnificent tomb, adorned with blue-green tiles, over the grave. Pilgrims poured in from far and near to pay homage to the saint. Their munificence enabled Nasreddin to raise a mosque around the tomb.

One day his master came past, having learned that his disciple had fulfilled his religious mission. He walked through a courtyard full of fountains, washed his feet and entered the mosque. The two men of God embraced each other. 'Allah is great,' exclaimed both in unison. 'Which saint is buried in the mosque?' asked the master. 'The ass you gave me when I left you. But tell me, which saint is buried in *your* mosque?' The master replied, 'The mother of your ass.'

VI: KEEPING YOUR HEAD

Nasreddin embodies the missing link between nature and culture. His actions are innocent and barbaric at the same time, holy and diabolic, ruthless and calculated. The holy fool combines hypersensitivity with insensitivity, bloodthirstiness with *sang-froid*. On the one hand, he demonstrates not a trace of fear, compassion or regret; on the other, he has an unshakable sense of honour. If necessary he will walk over corpses to prove his point.

Nasreddin had a regular table outside the teahouse. Every day a boy would run past and whip the turban off Nasreddin's head. The owner of the teahouse asked why Nasreddin did nothing about it. 'All in good time,' said Nasreddin. One day, a soldier was sitting in Nasreddin's place when the boy ran past and whipped the fur cap off the soldier's head. The soldier picked up his sword and cut the boy's head off. 'You see what I mean?' said Nasreddin.

VII: FIFTY LASHES

Nasreddin combined impetuous behaviour with unyielding logic. He persisted obstinately in his ways, as if the whole of creation depended on it, deaf and blind to arguments for and against. Yet there was method in his madness.

Nasreddin had brought good news for the sultan, but the chamberlain would only permit him to enter in exchange for half the remuneration he would receive. Nasreddin agreed and went inside. The sultan was delighted with the good news and told Nasreddin to choose his reward. 'Fifty lashes, if you please.'

THE ENLIGHTENED FOOL

Nasreddin set to work with the ruthlessness of a scientist who tortures nature in order to plumb her secrets; with the remorselessness of the astrologer who has divined the date of his own death and commits suicide on the day in question; with the fanaticism of the saint who offers up his family and his health for the sake of a dogma, and with the *sang-froid* of the horror-film heroine who descends alone into a cellar having heard a strange noise.

The fool is not the man who neglects his duty for the sake of private pleasures, but one who obstinately follows his path even if it clearly runs counter to his own best interests. Most dangerous is the enlightened fool who pursues his objective coldly, calmly and collectedly.

MOROSOPHY

Nasreddin's folly is not some kind of error, no breach of some rule, but poses a direct threat to the established order because it undermines standard thought patterns from within. His folly is a travesty. Nasreddin exposes the incongruity of all the moral and practical categories on which the established order is based by carrying them to absurd lengths. He turns thrift into avarice, piety into bigotry, diligence into overzealousness. He projects himself into the reasoning of the theologian, the politician, the farmer, and so on, the better to undermine received wisdom in an intelligent way. His folly amounts to the suicide of thought.

However, this negative picture has a positive side, for once the snake has swallowed itself, new wisdom prevails. The outsider reveals the essence of the established order. Wisdom is a folly that assumes the form of its opposite, sanctified stupidity. Every kind of logic is its own caricature, stupidity become reason, morosophy.

4 CLINAMEN

THE CATASTROPHE

How did animals, safe in their natural environment, governed by the rhythm of nature (the cycle of day and night, summer and winter, growth and decay), degenerate into man, who haunts the ruins of his symbolic universe like a homeless wraith?

According to the New Age commonplace, the original sin of Western civilization is man's arrogant belief that he is the centre of the universe and hence entitled to exploit all other creatures. This hubris, which upsets the unstable equilibrium of the cosmic forces, urges nature to restore harmony sooner or later. Our ecological, social and mental crisis is the revenge of the universe for man's pretensions. The only acceptable alternative is the holistic attitude by which we humbly accept our subordinate place in the great chain of being, a return to the 'old wisdom'.

The joke is, of course, that man's existence points to a disruption that is 'older' than wisdom. In other words: the 'old wisdom' was nothing but stupidity.

Stupidity is no psychological or medical category, no deficiency, deviation or illness that drives us to self-destruction. Stupidity is the ontological condition of human existence. Thanks to a catastrophe, there is something rather than nothing. Man is fundamentally unhinged.

THE MYTH

The cliché of the structurally unhinged man (St Augustine speaks of *natura sauciata*) inspires politicians on the Left to celebrate the destructive forces which defy the rules that throttle us, while it inspires

Title-page woodcut for *The Castle of Knowledge* (London, 1556), a book on astronomy by the Welsh scientist Robert Recorde. In the centre is the Castle of Knowledge. On the towers to either side we see figures using an astrolobe and a quadrant to observe the celestial bodies. In the foreground stand Fatum and Fortuna. Fatum (on the left) incorporates Destiny, man's future determined by the gods. Fortuna represents the vagaries of fate, the unpredictable future. Fatum holds a measuring compass in one hand and an armillary sphere in the other; the sphere of destiny is ruled by knowledge. Fortuna is holding a rein in one hand and in the other a rope attached to the wheel of fortune, ruled by ignorance. 'All who rise will speedily fall down', reads the wheel. The verse in the scroll tells us that while Earth is governed by time and chance, the celestial bodies follow an immutable and steady course. The study of the heavens, the treasury of knowledge and truth, helps man to avoid the whims of fortune. The astronomer can predict events and prepare us for them. The only problem is that our destiny does not manifest itself until our projects have been completed. It is then that our stupidity, negligence and ignorance round on us, and all our knowledge proves to be no more than a castle built on sand.

politicians on the Right to clamour for an authoritarian leader able to curb excess.

However, those who define man as an unhinged animal tacitly assume that nature is a deterministic realm of remorseless natural laws, or else a spiritual whole of cosmic forces thrown out of balance by man's arrogance.

All of them ignore the fact that there is no such thing as nature.

DUMB LUCK

The existence of the universe bears witness to a catastrophe: something emerged from nothing by upsetting an equilibrium. Aleatory materialism holds that the universe arose from the chance deflection of falling atoms, from a clinamen (Lucretius, *De rerum natura*, II, 217–24). The regular occurrence of solar eclipses is not evidence for some natural order, but for a chance event. A series of phenomena with a good chance of causing chaos adopts a regular form for no good reason. Order is a particular case of disorder. The world is characterized by the relative stability of certain atomic combinations. Every form of life enshrines catastrophe. The smallest variation can spell the end of civilization. At any one moment, nature can become unhinged by human interventions or as a result of her own unpredictable logic.

A clinamen is a precarious principle that disowns itself, since chance can never be the object of scientific demonstration.

IDIOCY

The ubiquity of dumb luck is bound up with the concept of idiocy (in its original Greek meaning of uniqueness). Everything that exists is unique in time and space, and hence unthinkable. Idiocy leaves no clues. It can only be indicated by itself – this is this, and that is that. Here we see the cause of the failure of interpretation, for every explanation involves something else, which must in turn be guaranteed by something else, and so on. In short, our thinking has to choose between tautology and error, between exchanges of banalities and stepping into the labyrinths of the Elsewhere and the Otherwise. Things can only be grasped with concepts that explain nothing but

Anonymous, 'Pons asinorum', 1678, copper engraving pasted in a notebook of 1678

The bridge is a didactic representation of the syllogistic figures of scholastic logic. With mnemonics the student can reach the other side, but anyone wishing to move from F to B falls off the bridge and ends up in the pool where the asses swim about with all their prize possessions: playing-cards, dice, pipes, tennis rackets, musical instruments, etc.

their own artificiality. Which, incidentally, does not detract from the importance of theories: these are imaginary solutions, fruitful artifices, as civilization demonstrates.

DUPLICATION

> It is customary to refer to the unusual combination of dissonant elements as monsters: centaurs or chimeras were defined in that way for those who failed to understand them. I refer by monster to every original and inexhaustible form of beauty.
> Alfred Jarry

Montaigne rejects the idea of normality in nature. For lack of criteria enabling us to define standards, everything that exists is equally monstrous (a monster is that which has no place in the concept of nature). The world is idiotic, stupid, simple, foolish, without purpose or cause, inescapable, unique, inexplicable, illogical and intangible. The result is intellectual agitation. Guided by the principle of insufficient reality we fall prey to transcendental temptations. Because an idiotic object has nothing to offer us, our desires are directed towards what does not exist.

In their attempts to explain the world, metaphysicians come up with such unworldly principles as Idea, Spirit or Universal Soul. The world is seen as a defective reflection of some other world. Thanks to this duplication, existence ceases to be gratuitous and becomes open to interpretation.

The other reality, the precise co-ordinates of which are carefully kept secret, provides what is said to be lacking here and now. It is all reminiscent of Ariosto's *Orlando Furioso*, where everything lost on earth is stored away in a fissure on the moon – not only wasted action and days, but also reason:

> It was as 'twere a liquor soft and thin,
> Which, save well corked, would from the vase have drained;
> Laid up, and treasured various flasks within,
> Larger or lesser, to that use ordained. [. . .]
> Only of folly is no trace there found,
> It stays on earth to thrive and to abound.

Duplication provides us with an alibi for not having to face harsh reality. The world disappears behind the vision of what it could or should have been. Art and morality do not resist banality and evil, but rise up against the idiocy of existence, perceived as scandalous and unreliable.

The visible world is not real, and the real world is not visible, and that is the magic trick. The moonstruck metaphysicians do their utmost to keep a secret: that there is no secret to be kept.

NATURE, CHANCE AND ARTIFICE

The occult pillar of metaphysical systems is the fantasm of nature. Since time immemorial, nature has been contrasted with chance on the one hand and with artifice on the other. Nature is considered to be a closed system of cause and effect, which answers a biological or spiritual need. In this way baffling idiocy is kept at bay and the fear of chance happenings is warded off. It is reassuring to think that order and necessity underlie all things.

This idea of nature also has a moral function: nature is seen as a pure, spontaneous and innocent play of forces, corrupted by man's interventions. Under the motto of 'Back to nature' everything artificial is renounced.

But every attempt to escape from artificiality is artificial. Looked at carefully, the idea of nature is the most artificial of all artifices, while artifice is the most natural feature of man. Not nature and culture, but idiocy and artificiality govern our existence. That is why the sophists celebrate the appearance, the effect and the moment.

KAIROS

> Art is long, life short, chance fleeting.
> Hippocrates, *Aphorisms*

The Greek word *kairos* refers to the unexpected ways in which things arise. Every order is the product of a chance concurrence of circumstances. The Greeks conferred divine status on the opportune moment: Kairos has wings on her ankles and shoulders and her head is plentifully covered with hair at the front and bald at the back. We must seize the opportunity when it appears. In her left hand she holds a razor on which rests a balance; with her right index finger she feels to see if the balance is dipping – *momentum* in Latin. Opportunity can cut deep when the moment is ripe. Kairos can turn honour into shame, loss into gain, fortune into misfortune, and vice versa. At the right moment it is sweet to play the fool – *dulce est desipere in loco* (Horace, *Odes*, IV.XII 27).

The Sophists tell us that life is a succession of exceptional opportunities, which have to be grasped when they arise. They embrace life in its full idiocy as an adventure in which everything is possible. They take pleasure in the inconstancy, the temporary character and the transience of existence. For the improviser life is one big surprise party.

5 'PATAPHYSICS

THE SCIENCE OF IMAGINARY SOLUTIONS

> I bet my life that he'll be peering
> Down a dark path, while nearing
> A ha-ha hidden from the eyes of all
> And into which he's bound to fall.
> Piron

'Pataphysics is the study of imaginary solutions devised by the French writer Alfred Jarry (1873–1907). It feeds on metaphysical concepts, scientific discoveries and technical achievements. Among other things, Jarry conceived a decerebration machine, developed Perpetual Motion Food, and computed the surface of God.

Jarry was not inspired by science alone, but also heeded the counsel of foolosophers. Victor Fournié, who claimed that the same sound had the same meaning in all languages, persuaded Jarry that IN-DUS-TRY stands for one-two-three in all languages.

'Pataphysics hinges on six principles:

1 'Pataphysics is the study of the particular, 'no matter how prevalent the idea that science is about the general'. Jarry did not look for similarities between phenomena, but for differences. Rightly considered, every phenomenon is exceptional. Rules are nothing but exceptions to exceptions, 'and not even the most original of these, because they occur so frequently'. The universe is the 'exception of itself'.

 'Pataphysics involves the microanalysis of the drop of water that causes the bucket to overflow, of the last straw that causes the heavily laden camel to buckle at the knees, of the one hair left before baldness sets in – all this in search of the laws of deviation.

According to 'Pataphysics there are no such things as normality and abnormality; all happenings are equally idiotic.

'Pataphysics is the study of epiphenomena; it discerns the beauty of monstrosity. Take London. The scientist who sets out to describe as complex a phenomenon as the city of London spreads a thin net of connections over reality, but the particular character of London slips through the meshes. 'Pataphysics is concerned with the monstrosities and miracles lurking in the gaps of our knowledge.

Immanuel Kant defined stupidity as a lack of judgement and wit. The fool is unable to bridge the gap between theory and practice; he is blind to exceptions to the rule, and unable to detect a new rule to a deviation. The pataphysicist by contrast, is able, like the sophist and the humorist, to bundle heterogeneous ideas under a single heading.

2   'Pataphysics is the study of imaginary solutions. Jarry exploits the possibilities that lie hidden in reality. He objects to ready-made opinions, and wonders why we think of a watch as round when every watch is rectangular if viewed from the side.

In 1950 the pataphysicist Raymond Queneau published a treatise entitled *Some summary remarks on the aerodynamic properties of sums*. 'In none of the attempts to prove that $2 + 2 = 4$, has the speed of the wind been taken into account.' The problem is that during a violent storm a number can topple over and the little cross can be blown away, with the result that $2 = 4$. The practical inference is: the moment one is afraid of atmospheric disturbances, it is best to give one's sums an aerodynamic shape.

'Pataphysics considers all theories, scientific or otherwise, as so many more or less unsuccessful attempts to come to terms with idiocy.

3   'Pataphysics explodes the common belief in what really exists and what does not. (Since when has fantasy been unreal?) Hence 'Pataphysics provides a glimpse of a parallel world, no less real than our own.

In the motion picture *The Romance of the Book and the Sword*, the contestants leap 100 feet into the air from a standing start, cross sabres after several saltos, before tumbling back to the ground. While fighting, they run up the walls of a tower, carefully avoiding the stairs. A leaflet that accompanied the film explained that the force of gravity plays a subordinate role in Zen Buddhism.

'Pataphysics treats metaphysics and physics as branches of fantasy fiction.

4   'Pataphysics turns accepted points of view upside down. Instead of the law of gravity, which states that all bodies fall towards a centre, Jarry postulates that emptiness (understood as non-density) rises to the periphery.

We learn by imitation, but if we suppose that imitation precedes the model, that the ideal is a perfect caricature, then parodies become so many guarantees of spiritual development.

5   'Pataphysics questions the identity principle and postulates the unity of opposites. In the pataphysical novel *Gestes et opinions du Docteur Faustroll, pataphysician. Roman néo-scientifique* (published posthumously in 1911), the all-round scholar Faustroll is accompanied by Bosse-de-Nage, a stupid Belgian with a baboon's buttocks for a head, who keeps interrupting his master's explanations with the tautological monosyllable, 'haha'.

> In the first instance, it is more judicious to use the orthography AA, for the aspiration *h* was never written in the ancient languages of the world. [. . .] A juxtaposed to A, with the former obviously equal to the latter, is the formula of the principle of identity: a thing is itself. It is at the same time the most excellent refutation of this very proposition, since the two A's differ in space, when we write them, if not indeed in time, just as two twins are never born together - even when issuing from the obscene hiatus of the mouth of Bosse-de-Nage.
>
> (*Translation*: Simon Watson Taylor)

If pronounced quickly, Haha illustrates the idea of unity; pronounced slowly, it illustrates the ideas of duality, echo, distance, symmetry, size and duration and the principle of good and evil.

The presence of Bosse is essential to Faustroll's philosophical views, and can no more be omitted from them than the apparently meaningless retort of the interlocutors in Socratic dialogues ('That is correct, Socrates.' 'Indeed.' 'You are telling the truth.'). This stopgap contains the essence of 'Pataphysics.

The principle of the unity of opposites has two consequences:

5a 'Pataphysics pays tribute to universal analogy. If A is both A and not-A, it may well be B, C or D, etc. The God of love is a vindictive God, and, who knows, perhaps the Devil incarnate. Law is legalized crime, freedom is slavery, dictatorship is anarchy, and knowledge is rationalized stupidity.

It follows that all views of the world are equally legitimate – the realist, no less than the symbolist, the materialist, the psychoanalytic, and so forth. Jarry's decerebration machine can represent loss of memory, senility, dementia praecox, but can also be an instrument of torture, a medical apparatus, a printing-press, a machine producing stultifying texts or an apparatus for ridding us of oppressive ideas.

5b 'Pataphysics upholds the principle of indifference. Everything is equally valuable or equally worthless. The pataphysician does not take sides. He is not above worldly confusion, but travels the world with an interested eye for everything that crosses his path. Every object is a potential source of reverie. He makes motley collections, orders objects without arriving at any order, leaves a trail of imaginary constructions. The pataphysician is opposed to a general consensus and champions one-man science.

The pataphysician is no sceptic. Anyone who claims that there is no neutral point from which to test the truth of our conclusions is a know-it-all *par excellence*. The pataphysician has changed the fixed point for a dynamic one that resolves or fuses all antitheses and categorical subdivisions; as a result all the comic takes on something sad, and the tragic something comic. And whenever he adopts a definite position, it is patently absurd.

The opposite of 'Pataphysics is pataphysics. Every idea is consciously or unconsciously pataphysical. Chance cannot be influenced, so that philosophy must be denied all practical application. However, 'Pataphysics does not take arms against ideologies, but treats all theories as equivalent reactions to the idiocy of existence. 'Pataphysics proclaims *a contrario* a truth that has the advantage of ridding us of even more absurd delusions. What we learn from it is to unlearn. Everything regains its bewildering character.

THE TWO SIDES OF THE APPLE

According to the Church Fathers, creation is a chain of beings running from Lucifer, via seraphs, cherubs, archangels, men, animals, plants and flowers to stones and minerals. God created the world out of chaos for the sake of man's happiness.

Two events put an end to this cosmic order, in which man played a central role. Lucifer, the highest-ranking angel, reached for omnipotence and was cast into the nether regions by God. On the way, he tempted Adam and Eve to eat of the forbidden fruit, whereupon they were banished from Paradise. (The vertical and horizontal expulsions are said to foreshadow Christ's crucifixion.) The turnabout at the top and at the centre of Creation brought about a change at all levels. Ever since, no one has known his place and role in the structure as a whole. The sin of pride opened the door to disorder. The world became a *mundus perversus*.

By eating the fruit of the knowledge of good and evil, man lost not only his innocence but also his grip on nature. In an attempt to repair the moral and scientific consequences of the Fall, we developed two universal instruments: satire and the encyclopædia.

THE COURAGE OF DESPAIR

Satire tries to restore order in the fallen world by pushing all perversities to extremes. To that end it makes use of humour and paradox. In prints depicting the world turned upside down we see pigs skinning the butcher, the blind leading the sighted, the sick tending the healthy. By exaggerating wrongs, satire points indirectly to the neglected order.

Encyclopædias, too, start from a lost harmony of which man was the centre. Before his vision was dimmed by sin, Adam was able to name the essence of things directly; everything bore witness to itself. Primitive speech perished in the Babylonian confusion of tongues. (Hebrew may resemble the *lingua adamica* most closely, but the morosopher Jan van Gorp proved in the sixteenth century that Dutch was the language spoken in Paradise, or rather Diets – medieval Dutch – and the Antwerp dialect in particular.)

Francis Bacon, the father of the modern encyclopædia, considered it his religious duty to help man regain power over nature with the help of the scientific method. He rejected all scholastic systems that forced the universe into ready-made schemes. People who present their fantasies as models of the world dishonour God's creation. Bacon replaced 'theatrical idols', which are as false as they are sinful, with observation and experiment. Nature is an open book to those who attempt to read her without preconceptions. Bacon developed an encyclopædic model of human knowledge, not the sum of all truths, not some mirror reflecting the absolute, but a fallible instrument designed to discover the forms with which nature is built, much as a language is built up with the letters of the alphabet. Only through the writings of nature can we be made privy to the mysteries of life and death.

According to Edward Topsell, Bacon's contemporary, natural history is a chronicle 'made by God himself, every living Beast being a word, every Kind being a sentence, and all of them together a large history, containing admirable knowledge and learning, which was, which is, which shall continue, (if not forever) yet to the World's end' (from *The Historie of Fore-footed Beastes and of Serpents*, 1607–8, quoted in David Knight, *Ordering the World*, London 1981, p. 61). It is the task of the encyclopædist to reconstruct this lost chronicle.

Paradoxically, the great story of nature disappeared behind the alphabetic division of knowledge introduced by Bacon's successors. The alphabet hints at a systematic approach but is completely arbitrary. In the nature of things, only an encyclopædia of the alphabet justifies an alphabetic sequence. If encyclopædias want to transcend the summation of isolated facts, then separate articles must contain cross-references to other articles. In that way the universe can be reconstructed along rational lines. The compiler organizes the available information into a clear and cohesive picture of the world in the firm conviction that time will impose order on our knowledge,

A tree-trunk sawing the woodcutter in half, from *Topsy-turvy World* (Munich, 1851)

which in turn will shape history itself. Satire and encyclopædias alike aim to convey a comprehensive and systematic picture of the world. Encyclopædias set out to reproduce the cosmic order faithfully and to scale. Classical satire, by contrast, paints a world stood on its head.

In fact, the failure of both genres is determined by their very objective. Seeing that all creation is cursed, the satirist has to mock everything and everybody, himself and his endeavours included, while the encyclopædist transforms the world he has set out to map.

THE SPECTRE OF ENCYCLOPÆDIAS

Satire and the encyclopædia, the two classical weapons against stupidity, have been in poor health since the beginning of the twentieth century.

Encyclopædias have fallen victim to the flood of knowledge they themselves have unleashed. They can no longer cope with the growing amount of information and the increasing difficulty of digesting it. The belief that progress would create order in our knowledge and lead to a possible synthesis has gone by the board. Encyclopædias were found to lack a co-ordinating method for systematizing often conflicting information. The accumulation of knowledge has led to stupefaction. The material overwhelmed the spirit and became as infinite and intricate as existence itself. Encyclopædias have ended up where they started, but with one great difference: from an inspiring chaos full of unrealized possibilities, they have been stranded on a stultifying heap of rubble, where alternatives prove to be so many obstacles. The ruins are haunted by the spectre of stupidity.

The sole remaining purpose of encyclopædias is vulgarization. The times when someone could change his view of the world by reading an encyclopædia are long past. Once symbols of man's faith in progress, they have degenerated into symbols of backwardness, eighteen-inch outsize volumes bound in imitation leather, decorations for wall units, with a replica of Rodin's *Thinker* as a choice bookend. The myth of knowledge has been interred, and is now celebrated with a globe of the world lit from within and a fountain pen as liturgical objects.

THE SPECTRE OF SATIRE

These developments also had repercussions on morality. Unlike encyclopædias, which pin their faith in the future, satire looks to the past, with the result that the gap between knowledge and morality has widened considerably. Satire itself has contributed to the anomie it set out to combat. As a reaction to growing intellectual confusion, more and more dichotomies were introduced that have done nothing but add to man's moral turmoil. Such concepts as good and evil kept changing their meaning. The contradictions could no longer be synthesized into a higher truth. Satire lost its corrective function because the norms on which it was based have themselves become ambivalent.

How can abuses be exposed when there is no longer any fixed point from which satire can tilt at reality? On which axis can the world be turned upside down? How can the world be stood on its head when it has become headless? Dolly Parton and Sylvester Stallone bear witness to the fact that caricature can no longer be distinguished from the ideal.

Satire and encyclopædias have become impotent. Both make desperate attempts to cope with diffusion, but morality and method fail to do so. Only stupidity continues to flourish. That is why satire and encyclopædias must band together: hence *The Encyclopædia of Stupidity*.

THE ENCYCLOPÆDIA OF THE STUPIDITY OF ENCYCLOPÆDIAS

As satire, *The Encyclopædia of Stupidity* questions the prevailing norms and hence its own foundations. Instead of dwelling on the contrast between good and evil, it assigns a crucial role to ambivalence, assailing morality on the one hand but serving as a source of humour on the other. Satire uses ambivalence as an ironic device aimed at all the old and new myths which seek to gloss over incongruities.

As an encyclopædia, *The Encyclopædia of Stupidity* concerns the failure of all our attempts to render existence intelligible. It no longer treats religion, metaphysics and science as milestones in the development of our knowledge, but as atemporal phenomena. Even historiography, long the religion of encyclopædias, is treated as one of many vain attempts to come to grips with perennial idiocy.

The contradictions can only be reconciled in the spectacle that has been made of them – hence an encyclopædia of the stupidity of encyclopædias. Totalization only succeeds in the successful portrayal of its own failures. In this way *The Encyclopædia of Stupidity* enjoys a coherence that its 'positive' sisters can only dream of attaining.

To stay alive, encyclopædias must no longer concentrate on the accumulation of knowledge but on the development of an essayistic method by which we can come to terms with the world. The essayist practices vivisection on existence; he analyses reality in order to trip up certainties on the one hand and to try out alternatives on the other. He faces everyday life as if it were an experiment, a laboratory in which living forms are put to the test. Every truth is a possible truth.

THE SYRUP

Satire no longer inverts reality but renders tangible the inversion lurking in our self-evident world. Satire demonstrates that everything bad contains some good, and the other way around; in short that everything has been corrupted. Fantasy is unmasked as fantasy and idiocy laid bare. Not in order to eradicate stupidity – stupidity is ineradicably human. Its elimination would be inhuman. It is indeed by incorporating stupidity that morality remains tolerant. In the method used, satire demonstrates that the essential is to be found precisely in incessant attempts to grasp the self-destructive obverse of our attempts to render existence intelligible.

The Encyclopædia of Stupidity seeks the truth in the sum of contradictions, where the comical too has its roots. It strives for a syrupy ambiguity in the hope that a new meaning may crystallize.

THE CHOREOGRAPHY OF KNOWLEDGE AND MORALITY

Both encyclopædias and satire once had a pedagogic objective. The term 'encyclopædia' is of Greek origin. The twelfth-century Byzantine scholar John Tzetzes states in his didactic poem Chiliades that enkyklios originally referred to the lyrical chorus and only secondarily to a closed circle of knowledge. According to the Pythagoreans, the musical declamation of poetic wisdom with rhythmical accompaniment leads to an understanding of the interrelationship, harmony and proportion of all that exists, which, in its turn, leads to a harmony of the soul. Choral training (enkyklios paideia) leads man from the visible to the invisible.

Satire, too, looks for real existence behind the world of appearances. In the Dance of Death, members of all estates – from monarch to peasant – are swept away. In the face of death everyone is equal. Not only is the vanity of all human structures unmasked in the danse macabre, but the Apocalypse also signifies the unveiling of the celestial hierarchy.

Between the two genres there is also a great difference. Encyclopædias set out to inform the ignorant and the superstitious; they are by nature future-orientated and optimistic. Satire, in its turn, sets out to redeem sinful man and lead him back to an ideal order rooted in the past, in which everyone knew his task and his place. In essence, satire is pessimistic; it secretly believes in man's incorrigible sinfulness.

The Encyclopædia of Stupidity by contrast is neither happy nor sad. It observes with amazement the successful flops that all in all constitute our civilization. It looks for essence in appearance; there is no truth beyond man's vain hunt for the truth. For that reason it dances a modest two step with its own shadow.

KNOW THYSELF

207

Acknowledgements

The translators have gratefully made use of the following sources (among many others), occasionally altering them very slightly to fit in with the text of this book.

Aristophanes, *The Frogs*, trans. J. Hookham Frere (London, 1949)
Isaac Asimov, 'Franchise', in *Robot Dreams* (London, 1997)
Edmund Burke, *A Philosophical Enquiry into the Origin of Our Ideas of the Sublime and Beautiful* (Oxford, 1990)
Samuel Butler, *Hudibras* (London, 1663–78)
Elias Canetti, *Auto-da-Fé*, trans. C. V. Wedgwood (London, 2000)
Cebes of Thebes, *The Tabula of Cebes* (Chico, CA, 1983)
Carlo Collodi and Lee Hall, *The Adventures of Pinocchio* (London, 2001)
Dante Alighieri, *The Divine Comedy*, trans. H. F. Cary (Gutenberg Project)
T. S. Eliot, *The Hollow Men* (London, 1925)
Lucretius, *On the Nature of Things*, metrical trans. by W. E. Leonard (Gutenberg Project)
Bernard Mandeville, *The Fable of the Bees* (London 1970)
John Milton, *Paradise Lost* (New York, 1968)
Jean-Jacques Rousseau, *The Social Contract and the Discourses*, trans. G.D.H. Cole (London, 1993)
Horace Walpole, *The History of the Modern Taste in Gardening*, intro. John Dixon Hunt (New York, 1995)

Acknowledgements for the following photos: p. 36 (Roos Aldershof), p. 71 (E. van Moerkerken), p. 190 (Universiteitsbibliotheek Leuven).

FORTHCOMING

FROM REAKTION BOOKS

A Philosophy of Boredom

Lars Svendsen

We all get bored from time to time. For lots of people it's *all* the time. But what, exactly, is boredom? Where does it come from? Where does it go? *Why* do we get bored?

In this brilliant new book the philosopher Lars Svendsen investigates what Dostoevsky called 'a bestial and indefinable affliction'. He explains how boredom originated, how and why it afflicts us, and why we cannot seem to overcome it by any act of will. He brings together philosophy, literature, psychology, theology and popular culture, examining boredom's pre-Romantic manifestations in medieval torpor and related modern concepts of alienation and transgression, taking in texts by Samuel Beckett, J. G. Ballard, Andy Warhol and many others.

This thoughtful and entertaining book considers a serious issue. It will appeal to anyone who has ever felt bored, and wanted to know why.

UK £14.95 RRP
US $24.95
paperback original

ISBN 1 86189 217 9